CHECK YOUR ENGLISH VOCABULARY FOR

BUSINESS

AND

ADMINISTRATION

Fourth edition

Rawdon Wyatt

A & C Black • London

www.acblack.com

FARNHAM COLLEGE
Morley Road • Farnham • Surrey • GU9 8LU
Telephone 01252 716988   Fax 01252 723969

First published as *Check Your Vocabulary for Business* in 1996
by Peter Collin Publishing
Second edition published 1999
Third edition published 2003
by Bloomsbury Publishing Plc

This fourth edition published 2007 by
A & C Black Publishers Ltd
38 Soho Square, London W1D 3HB
Reprinted 2008

© Rawdon Wyatt 2007

A CIP entry for this book is available from the British Library
ISBN-10: 0-7136-7916-6
ISBN-13: 978-0-7136-7916-8

Text typeset by A & C Black
Printed in Great Britain at Caligraving Ltd, Thetford, Norfolk

This book is produced using paper that is made from wood grown in managed, sustainable forests. It is natural, renewable and
recyclable. The logging and manufacturing processes conform to the environmental regulations of the country of origin.

If you want to practise and develop your knowledge of English vocabulary for Business and Administration, you will find that the exercises in this book will help you. They are particularly useful if:

- You work, or are planning to work, in or around an English-speaking business environment.
- Your work brings you into regular contact with English-speaking business people.
- You are planning to take a Business English examination such as BEC Vantage / Higher, TOEIC, or one of the LCCI (London Chamber of Commerce and Industry) International Qualifications, especially 2nd, 3rd or 4th level Business.
- You do not work directly in Business and Administration, but your job requires you to have a working knowledge of common business words and expressions.

If you want to make the most of the exercises in the book, you should note the following:

- This is not a course book, and you do not need to work through it 'mechanically' from beginning to end. It is better to choose areas that you are unfamiliar with, or areas that you feel are of specific interest or importance to you.
- Write down new words and expressions that you learn. Develop your own personal vocabulary 'bank' in a notebook or file. Review these words and expressions on a regular basis so that they become a part of your 'productive' vocabulary.
- Use a good general-English dictionary and a good business-English dictionary to check the meanings of new words and expressions (but try to do the exercises first before looking in the dictionary). Many of the examples in this book have been taken from the *Macmillan English Dictionary* (ISBN 978-0-333-96847-5) and the A&C Black *Dictionary of Business* 4th edition (ISBN 978-0-713-67918-2).
- The exercises in this book either focus on *general* business vocabulary (for example, phrasal verbs, formal words, words with similar meanings, etc) or *topic-specific* business vocabulary (for example, sales and marketing, recruitment, dispute resolution, etc). However, you should be aware that not all of the vocabulary is exclusive to business and administration, and not all of the topic-specific vocabulary is exclusive to that particular topic. For example, 'commission' appears in the section on *Earnings, rewards and benefits*, but it could also be applied to *Sales and marketing*.
- The key at the back of the book not only has answers for all of the exercises, but also provides you with other relevant information. For example, it gives you alternative answers, provides more words and expressions that are not featured in the exercises themselves, explains what some of the words and expressions mean, and elaborates on some of the topic areas
- The book does not contain every single word or expression that you are likely to meet or to need. You should therefore try to develop your vocabulary further by reading from a variety of other resources, such as newspapers, magazines, journals and books. As a reference source, the author particularly recommends *Business – The Ultimate Resource*, published by A&C Black (ISBN 978-0-713-67509-2).

We hope that you enjoy doing the exercises in this book, and that they help you to practise and develop the Business and Administration vocabulary that you need.

Contents

Test your knowledge of business abbreviations and acronyms. Look at these abbreviations, then complete the crossword grid on the next page with the words that are missing from their complete forms.

Across (⇨)

2. EU = _____ Union.
4. MBO = management _____ *(the letters B and O are used in one word)*
8. USP = unique _____ point.
9. AOB = any other _____.
11. PEST analysis = political, social, economic and _____ analysis.
13. MD = Managing _____.
14. ROI = return on _____.
15. M & A = _____ and acquisitions.
17. OTE = on-target _____.
19. PAYE = pay as you _____.
20. VAT = Value Added _____.
22. SWOT analysis = strengths, weaknesses, _____ and threats analysis.
25. CEO = Chief _____ Officer.
26. CV = curriculum _____.
27. TNA = trainee _____ analysis.
29. TOIL = _____ off in lieu.
32. RRP = recommended retail _____.
34. CFO = Chief _____ Officer.
37. FAQ = frequently asked _____.
38. RSI = repetitive strain _____.
39. RPI = retail price _____.
41. p.a. = per _____.
43. APR = _____ percentage rate.
45. ICC = International Chamber of _____.
49. FYI = for your _____.
51. NPD = new _____ development.
52. SET = _____ electronic transaction.
54. GDP = gross _____ product.
56. VIP = very important _____.

Down (⇩)

1. TQM = total _____ management.
3. PPP = purchasing power _____.
5. PLC = _____ limited company.
6. AGM = annual general _____.
7. PR = public _____.
10. L/C = letter of _____.
12. MBA = Master of Business _____.
15. O & M = organization and _____.
16. HR = human _____.
18. POS = point of _____.
21. P & L statement = _____ and loss statement.
23. ASAP = as soon as _____.
24. CBD = _____ business district.
28. COD = cash on _____.
30. LIFO = last in, _____ out.
31. NVQ = National Vocational _____.
33. GNP = gross _____ product.
35. NI = National _____.
36. CPD = continuing professional _____.
40. ESOP = employee _____ ownership plan.
42. In £20K, K means _____.
44. EFT = _____ funds transfer.
46. R & D = _____ and development.
47. P & P = _____ and packing.
48. ISP = _____ service provider.
50. FOB = _____ on board.
53. IOU = I owe _____. *(Be careful: the word you need does not begin with the letter u)*
55. JIT production = Just-in-_____ production.

For reference see *Dictionary of Business - 4th edition* (A&C Black Publishers Ltd, 978-0-713-67918-2)

2

Appraisals, training and staff development

Exercise 1: Look at the common employee appraisal questions in 1 – 28, and complete each one with a word from the box. These words can be found by reading from left to right and from right to left in the direction of the arrows (but they are not in the same order as the sentences they complete). Write your answers in the spaces on the right. The letter in the **bold** space in one word should be the same as the letter in the shaded space in the next word. Note that in some sentences there is more than one possible answer, but only one will fit into the space on the right. The first one has been done for you.

```
START ⇨  a d v a n c e m e n t c h a l l e n g i n g ⇨
 ⇦ d e n i f e d s t n i a l p m o c s t n e m m o c ⇦
 ⇨ d e s c r i p t i o n d i s c i p l i n e f a c i ⇨
 ⇦ n i v o r p m i t n e m e v o r p m i s e i t i l ⇦
 ⇨ g k n o w l e d g e l e a s t m o r a l e o b j e ⇨
 ⇦ r g o r p s s e r g o r p e s i a r p s e v i t c ⇦
 ⇨ e s s i o n p r o m p t l y p r o v i s i o n s q ⇨
 ⇦ h s n o i t a l e r d n e m m o c e r y t i l a u ⇦
 ⇨ i p s c h e d u l e **s t a n d a r d s** s t r e n g ⇨
 ⇦ l k r o w t n e m t a e r t g n i n i a r t s h t ⇦
 ⇦ o a d
```

1. Do you think the work you are doing meets or exceeds the correct _____ ?

   S T A N D A R D S

2. How far do you think you have the skills and _____ to achieve your duties?

   N

3. How would you describe the _____ of the work you are doing?

4. Do you feel you have met the work _____ that were set for you?

5. Do you think you have room for _____ ?

6. In your opinion, what are your main _____ and weaknesses?

7. Would you benefit from going on a _____ course?

8. Are you happy with your career _____ at the moment?

9. Do you feel you are able to manage your work _____ ?

10. Would you like to do something a bit more _____ ?

11. What do you like most and what do you like _____ about the job you are doing?

12. How do you feel about your _____ ? Can you deal with it?

For reference see *Dictionary of Business - 4th edition* (A&C Black Publishers Ltd, 978-0-713-67918-2)

13. Is your current job _____ accurate?

14. Are your job duties clearly _____?

15. Do you feel that there are enough opportunities for _____?

16. Do you have any suggestions for _____ your current job?

17. Are you happy with the _____ in your department?

18. Do you have a good working _____ with your colleagues?

19. Do you feel _____ is fair in your department?

20. Does your manager show you fair _____ at all times?

21. Does your manager deal _____ with problems, or does she ignore them?

22. Does your manager deal efficiently with staff _____ that may arise?

23. Does your manager inform you of any _____ you are making?

24. Does your manager give you _____ for work well done?

25. How do you feel about the _____ and services provided by the company?

26. Do you feel that the health and safety _____ are adequate?

27. Would you _____ this company as an employer to others?

28. Have you got any more _____ you would like to make?

This final letter is also the first letter of number 1 ✎

Exercise 2: Look at the different types of training courses and other aspects of staff development in the box, then match each one with a description in paragraphs 1 – 14 on the next page. Two courses in the box do not match any of the descriptions.

action learning	adventure learning	assertiveness training	carousel training
continuous personal development (CPD)		experiential learning	an induction course
in-tray learning	modern apprenticeship	off-the-job training	online learning
open learning	total quality management (TQM)	sales training	team-building
	training needs analysis (TNA)		

4

For reference see *Dictionary of Business - 4th edition* (A&C Black Publishers Ltd, 978-0-713-67918-2)

1. This company is committed to helping its employees learn about their jobs and develop their skills for the whole period they are working here, and not just at the beginning of their contract. We run regular courses and workshops in order to achieve this, both on and outside the company premises.

2. Our employees have to deal with a lot of difficult situations, and they often come in contact with people who can be difficult to work with and do business with. We train them to have more confidence in themselves so that they can deal effectively with any problems and difficulties they encounter.

3. We believe that the best way of learning a skill is through practice. We don't waste time on courses and workshops. We show the employee his duties, give him an outline of how the company operates, and then we just say 'Get on with it, and good luck'. It's a remarkably effective method.

4. It's very important that our employees develop skills in leadership, problem solving, decision-making and interpersonal communication. The best way to achieve this is to get them involved in group games and physically demanding outdoor activities like sailing and climbing. These also help to build team spirit.

5. When we promote somebody to a management position, the first thing we do is to give them a lot of typical management paperwork and tell them to deal with it. We set them a time limit for this, and monitor them carefully to see how they get on. We then review their performance and show them where they went right or wrong.

6. Our company understands how important it is that our employees work well together in order for the company to be effective. Our training sessions are designed to instil co-operation and solidarity in a group of employees who have to work together.

7. It is our company policy to make sure that our employees know how all the jobs in the company work, not just their own. We find the best way of doing this is to move them from job to job and department to department. They meet colleagues who they might not normally meet, and learn about their jobs and how they operate.

8. New employees in our company need to learn about our products and how they work, how the distribution system operates, how to deal with both suppliers and customers and how to handle complaints. They also study trade and retail laws, and are accompanied on their first customer visits by their trainer.

9. I've been interested in photography since I was very young, so when I finished school I started learning how to be a photographer. I spend my week working with a professional, who teaches me about all the different aspects of the job. At the same time, I receive training in areas such as numeracy, problem-solving and interpersonal skills.

10. First of all I was given a tour of the factory and then I was introduced to my colleagues and was given an outline of the company and its products. After that I was guided through the company's code of practice, taken to my department and shown my duties.

11. My company can't hold training workshops in the office because we don't have enough space, and of course while we are learning, we aren't actually making money, so the company feels it wouldn't be making the best use of its employees. Instead, they send us to a college in the evening where we develop our skills and knowledge.

12. This company believes that personal development and training should be more flexible. As a result, we have developed a system of flexible training courses that a trainee or employee can start at any time, and which does not require a teacher.

13. Once a year we look at the different skills and abilities of our staff, and we decide if they are enough to help the company fulfil its aims and operate effectively. We then develop a series of classes and workshops to help the staff learn more about their job and how they can operate more effectively.

14. This company has a policy that our managers should be committed to maintaining and improving the quality of their work, and also their skills and knowledge. We run courses, classes and workshops on a regular basis, and ensure that they are kept up to date with all the latest developments.

For reference see *Dictionary of Business - 4th edition* (A&C Black Publishers Ltd, 978-0-713-67918-2)

Changes

Exercise 1: Look at sentence pairs 1 – 22, then complete the second sentence in each pair with a word or expression from the box so that its meaning is similar to the first sentence. There are some words / expressions in the box that do not fit in any of the sentences. You do <u>not</u> need to change the form of any of the words / expressions.

amended	build up	considerable growth	constant rise	cuts	deterioration
downsizing	downward trend	dramatic increase	expansion		fluctuated
general improvement	marked progress	narrow	narrowing		phased in
phased out	reduce	relaxation	restructure	sharp decline / fall	
steady decrease	streamline	strengthening	tightening up		upgrade
upward trend	weakening	widening			

1.   Last year, 33% of the population worked in secondary industries and 48% worked in the tertiary sector. This year, the figures are 27% and 53% respectively.
     There has been a _____ of the gap between those working in different sectors of the economy.

2.   Last year, the overseas market accounted for 60% of our sales. This year, it only accounts for about 15%.
     There has been a _____ in overseas sales figures in the last year.

3.   People can afford to buy more and live more comfortably than they could twenty years ago.
     There has been a _____ in the standard of living.

4.   Because our company is bigger now than it was two years ago, we need to recruit more employees.
     Because of company _____ over the last two years, we need more workers.

5.   British travellers abroad have discovered that they can buy less foreign currency with their pound.
     There has been a _____ of the pound sterling.

6.   It is now much harder to import goods into the country than it was a few years ago.
     There has been a _____ of border controls for imports.

7.   In 2002 inflation was running at about 4%, in 2003 it was 4.5%, in 2004 it was 5% and in 2005 it was 5.5%.
     Between 2002 and 2005, there was a _____ in the rate of inflation.

8.   Last year, the company employed 200 people. This year it now has over 1000 employees.
     There has been a _____ in the number of employees working for the company.

9.   Unemployment figures have dropped by about 2% every year for the last four years.
     There has been a _____ in unemployment figures over the last four years.

10. Over the next few years, some management positions in the company will be gradually removed.
     Some management positions will be _____ over the next few years.

11. Because of forecasts for high demand in the future, we need to increase our stocks.
     We need to _____ our stocks to cope with future demand.

12. The government will spend less on import subsidies next year.
     There are going to be _____ in import subsidy spending next year.

13. Public services are less reliable now than they were five years ago.
     There has been a _____ in public services reliability over the last five years.

14. Nowadays, more and more people are travelling abroad for business and pleasure.
     There has been _____ in the overseas travel market.

For reference see *Dictionary of Business - 4th edition* (A&C Black Publishers Ltd, 978-0-713-67918-2)

15. Compared with five years ago, more people are shopping at out-of-town retail parks than in town centre shops.

    There has been an _____ in the number of people shopping in out-of-town retail parks.

16. Unless your work visibly improves, we will have to recommend a transfer to another department.

    We need to see some _____ in your work, or we will recommend a departmental transfer.

17. Over the next two months, we plan to make our office computers faster and more efficient.

    Over the next two months, we plan to _____ our office computers.

18. We are trying to make the accounting system simpler and more efficient.

    We are trying to _____ the accounting system.

19. Making the company smaller by making a lot of staff members redundant has made it much more profitable than it was before.

    _____ the company has made it much more profitable than it was before.

20. Property prices have gone up, then gone down, then gone up again twice this year.

    Property prices have _____ twice this year.

21. We have made small changes to the rules for applying for instant credit.

    We have _____ the rules for applying for instant credit.

22. The company is planning to change its marketing division to make it more effective.

    The company is planning to _____ its marketing division.

Exercise 2. Choose the most appropriate word in **bold** to complete sentences 1 – 10.

1. The company cannot refund customers' money, and goods can only be **altered / exchanged / revised** on production of a receipt or other proof of purchase.

2. We have made radical changes to the working regulations, and employees are expected to **expand / stretch / adapt** to these over the next few weeks.

3. Our customer call centre used to be in Sheffield, but last year we **promoted / varied / outsourced** it to India, where costs are much lower.

4 The new director has completely **reduced / transformed / heightened** the company, from a small local enterprise to a major international concern.

5. The hotel is currently being **renovated / replaced / switched** but will remain open while building work is carried out.

6. Production has been **switched / disappeared / enlarged** from our Bracknell site to a new industrial centre near Milton Keynes.

7. Our new memory cards **extend / vary / raise** in price, from £42 for a 64Mb card up to £140 for a 2Gb card.

8. The Internet clothing company Pants2U.com has **deepened / shortened / expanded** its range to include jewellery and watches.

9. The decision to **dissolve / demote / disappear** the company wasn't an easy one to make, but everyone agreed that there was no other option but to cease trading.

10. Air fares will be **adapted / extended / revised** on 21 July: domestic flights will go down by 10%, but international flights will go up by 22%.

7

For reference see *Dictionary of Business - 4th edition* (A&C Black Publishers Ltd, 978-0-713-67918-2)

Business 'colours'

Test your knowledge with this quiz.

1. Match the examples of different goods in (a) - (e) with the colours in the box that are often used by businesses to 'categorize' them.
    (a) A pair of trousers, a T-shirt and a cap.
    (b) A television set, a stereo and a DVD player.
    (c) A refrigerator, a dishwasher and a washing machine.
    (d) A car, an air-conditioning unit and a bathroom suite.
    (e) A carton of milk, 250g of cheese and a bottle of tomato ketchup.

    | white goods | brown goods | red goods | orange goods | yellow goods |

2. What is the informal expression given to paperwork which takes a long time to complete? Is it:
    (a) white noise   **(b)** yellow card   **(c)** green belt   **(d)** red tape   **(e)** blue ribbon

3. What is the difference between being *in the red* and being *in the black*?

4. Complete this sentence with one word: Goods and services which are paid for in cash, and therefore not declared for tax, are features of a _____ economy.

5. What is the name given to taxes that are levied to discourage behaviour that will damage the environment?

6. True or false: If you make a *blue-chip investment*, you buy high-risk shares in a company that is not performing very well.

7. Sometimes a company will not deal with a person or company, etc, because they have done something wrong and should be avoided. What is the name for this?
    (a) to blackball **(b)** to blacklist **(c)** to blackhead **(d)** to blackmail **(e)** to blackleg

8. A company owns some land in the country that has been designated as a *greenfield site*. Can it build a factory or warehouse on that land?

9. What is the difference between a *white-collar worker* and a *blue-collar worker*?

10. Complete this sentence: *Embezzlement, computer fraud* and *insider dealing* are examples of _____ crime.

11. Who might be offended if you described the work they did as a *pink-collar job*?

12. What is the name given to the buying and selling of goods or currency in a way which is not allowed by law?

13. The MD of your company often has *blue-sky ideas*. From a business point of view is this a good thing or a bad thing?

14. Your accountant tells you that the stocks and bonds you have recently bought are *blue-sky securities*. Would you feel happy or unhappy about this?

15. What is a *grey market*? Is it:
    (a) a market in which goods are sold that have been made abroad and then imported (legally), often as a result of reduced production of / increased demand for those goods in the market country
    b) an informal expression for the market segment occupied by older members of a population
    (c) the unofficial trading of securities that have not yet become available for trading on the Stock Exchange

For reference see *Dictionary of Business - 4th edition* (A&C Black Publishers Ltd, 978-0-713-67918-2)

Exercise 1: The text below gives a definition and brief explanation of what a contract is. Complete it with words or expressions from the box.

accepted	agreement	breach	consideration	contractual liability
damages	express	implied	intention	obligations offer
under seal	reward	signed	stated	sue terms
	verbally	voided	writing	

A contract can be defined as 'an _____ between two or more parties to create legal _____ between them'. Some contracts are made '_____': in other words, they are _____ and sealed (stamped) by the parties involved. Most contracts are made _____ or in _____. The essential elements of a contract are: (a) that an _____ made by one party should be _____ by the other; (b) _____ (the price in money, goods or some other _____, paid by one party in exchange for another party agreeing to do something); (c) the _____ to create legal relations. The _____ of a contract may be _____ (clearly stated) or _____ (not clearly _____ in the contract, but generally understood). A _____ of contract by one party of their _____ entitles the other party to _____ for _____ or, in some cases, to seek specific performance. In such circumstances, the contract may be _____ (in other words, it becomes *invalid*).

Exercise 2: Look at paragraphs 1 – 6 in the boxes, and answer the questions that follow them.

1.

> This contract is <u>binding</u>, and we expect all the <u>parts</u> involved (both clients *and* suppliers) to <u>abide by</u> the <u>terms and conditions</u> stated in sections 3a - 37g on pages 1 - 17.

1. One of the <u>underlined</u> words / expressions in the above sentence is wrong. Identify and correct it.
2. True or false: A contract which is *binding* is flexible and can be changed at any time.
3. Which of these words / expressions could replace *abide by*?:
   (a) choose   (b) agree with   (c) obey   (d) change

2.

> On <u>terminator</u> of this contract, the company will be <u>obliged</u> to return any unused materials to the supplier within 28 days, unless <u>provision</u> has been made for a temporary extension. If any of the rules of the contract are <u>broken</u>, all materials must be returned immediately.

1. One of the underlined words / expressions in the above sentence is wrong. Identify and correct it.
2. True or false: *Provision* has a similar meaning to *arrangement*.
3. Rearrange these letters to make two words which have a similar meaning to *obliged*:
   degabtlio   edequrir

3.

> The contract was originally <u>verbal</u>, but we've finally managed to get the company to give us something on paper. They say that this contract is <u>un-negotiable</u>, but maybe we can persuade them to <u>amend</u> some of the details before we sign <u>on the dotted line</u>.

For reference see *Dictionary of Business - 4th edition* (A&C Black Publishers Ltd, 978-0-713-67918-2)

1. One of the <u>underlined</u> words / expressions in the above paragraph is wrong. Identify and correct it.
2. True or false: The speaker thinks that it might be possible for small changes to be made to the contract before she signs it.
3. Rearrange the letters in **bold** to make four words which have the same meaning as *verbal* in this situation
   rola   kosnep   plidemi   etodnurdso

4.

> Swillpot Airline Catering Ltd were <u>sued</u> by Pan-Globe Airways when they were found to be <u>in beach of</u> their contract, specifically that they had failed to <u>comply with</u> <u>clause</u> 27B, which stated that their food should be "fit for human consumption".

1. One of the <u>underlined</u> words / expressions in the above sentence is wrong. Identify and correct it.
2. Find a word or expression in paragraphs 1 - 3 above which has a similar meaning to *comply with* in paragraph 4.
3. True or false: Pan-Globe Airways are unhappy with Swillpot Airline Catering because they have broken *all* of their contract.

5.

> Withers Interiors Ltd have entered into an <u>agreement</u> with Sophos Construction to act as sole providers of quality interior fittings <u>commencing</u> 15 August this year. This is to run for 18 months, with a 3 month <u>period of notification</u> in the event of <u>cancellation</u> by either side.

1. One of the <u>underlined</u> words / expressions in the above sentence is wrong. Identify and correct it.
2. Which word in the paragraph is the closest in meaning to the noun *contract*?
3. True or false: If either Withers Interiors Ltd or Sophos Construction want to end the contract, they must tell the other company 3 months before they do it.

6.

> This contract recognizes the <u>anointment</u> of Mr Alan Wiley as non-executve Director to the board of AKL Publishing following the company's <u>amalgamation</u> with Berryhill Books. While Mr Wiley may continue to buy stocks in the company, he may not acquire a <u>controlling interest</u>, and he may have no professional dealings with any <u>third parties</u> during this period.

1. One of the <u>underlined</u> words / expressions in the above sentence is wrong. Identify and correct it.
2. True or false: AKL Publishing recently separated from Berryhill Books.
3. Mr Wiley can buy as many shares as he likes in the company.
4. In addition to sitting on the board of AKL Publishing, how many other companies can Mr Wiley work for?

For reference see *Dictionary of Business - 4th edition* (A&C Black Publishers Ltd, 978-0-713-67918-2)

Dispute resolution

Exercise 1. Complete this text with words or expressions from the box.

abide by	action	breach	commercial	compensation	conditions
cost effective	decreased	disagreement	disinterested	dismissals	
go-slow	industrial	litigation	mediation	obligations	overtime
redundancy	regulations	strike	suit	terms	trade union	work-to-rule

A *dispute* is an argument or _____. In business and commerce, there are usually two types of dispute.

The first of these is an _____ dispute, which is between an employer and an employer's representative, which in many cases is a _____. These are usually the result of disagreements over pay, conditions of work and unfair _____, including _____ (the laying-off of employees because they are not needed). The least favourable outcome of this type of dispute is usually industrial _____, often in the form of a _____ (where employees stop working). Alternatively, employees may stage a _____ (where they work at less than their normal speed). They may also adopt a _____ strategy, in which they strictly follow all the _____ of their contract, and obey other _____ to the letter*. They may also refuse to work . The result of this is usually _____ productivity for the company.

The second type of dispute is a _____ dispute, which is a disagreement between two businesses. This is usually the result of a _____ of contract (in which one or both sides fails to agree to, or _____, the terms and _____ of a contract drawn up between them). In extreme cases, this may result in _____ (in which one side brings a _____ against the other in a court of law), with the aim of getting financial _____, or of legally obliging the other side to abide by their contractual _____.

Disputes do not necessarily have to be settled in an imposed court case. _____ (an attempt by a _____ third party to make two sides in an argument agree) is often quicker, more _____ and less stressful for the parties involved.

(* If you do or obey something *to the letter*, you do it very thoroughly, without making any mistakes.)

Exercise 2. Complete the first part of each word in **bold** in sentences 1 – 19 with the second part in the box. Some of the words have already appeared in Exercise 1.

____actually	____ain	____artial	____bunal	____cation	____closed
____cus	____dential	____ding	____ficial	____gation	____iator
____int	____itator	____judice	____lements	____lic	____native
____our	____promise	____sent	____sion	____tiations	____tical
____tration	____trator	____ual	____und	____untary	____utions

For reference see *Dictionary of Business - 4th edition* (A&C Black Publishers Ltd, 978-0-713-67918-2)

1. Mediation is one form of what is known as **alter**_____ *dispute resolution* (ADR for short).

2. Mediation is generally preferable to **liti**_____ because it is normally quicker and cheaper.

3. Mediation is **vol**_____, but requires the **con**_____ of all the parties involved before it can go ahead.

4. Mediation is carried out by a neutral, **imp**_____ third party called a **med**_____.

5. This third party is also sometimes known as a **facil**_____.

6. He / she spends time with all the parties involved in **jo**_____ **ses**_____ and also in private meetings (known as a '**cau**_____').

7. Any information that the parties provide is **confi**_____ and cannot be **dis**_____ to the other parties.

8. He / she attempts to solve problems and find **resol**_____ that are **prac**_____ and **bene**_____ to everyone.

9. Unlike a formal court case, **nego**_____ are in private.

10. Resolutions and **sett**_____ are based on **com**_____ and on **mut**_____ agreement and acceptance.

11. If no agreement is reached, the parties involved will not be legally **bo**_____ by anything that has been discussed.

12. A mediation process is said to be 'without **pre**_____', which means that anything that was said during the mediation cannot be used if there is no agreement and the case has to go to court.

13. If an agreement is reached and the parties sign a written agreement, this agreement becomes **bin**_____, and the parties are obliged to **hon**_____ it.

14. This signed agreement can then be enforced **contr**_____ if necessary.

15. Another form of dispute resolution is **arbi**_____.

16 This will involve all parties in the dispute appearing before a **tri**_____.

17. An **arbi**_____ is employed. He / she is usually an expert in a particular field, and so this form of dispute resolution may be preferable in disputes where specialist knowledge is required.

18. However, unlike mediation, this form of resolution involves an **adjudi**_____ which will probably benefit one side in the dispute more than the other(s).

19. This form of dispute resolution is also less private than mediation (each party is aware of what the other party is saying about it), and information may end up in the **pub**_____ **dom**_____.

Also see *Workplace problems* on pages 65-66.

For reference see *Dictionary of Business - 4th edition* (A&C Black Publishers Ltd, 978-0-713-67918-2)

Complete the first part of each word in **bold** in sentences 1 – 34 with the second part in the box.

-an	-ance	-ance	-ans	-ary	-ated	-ation	-ay	-ble	-ck	
-count	-ction	-dancy	-den	-dex	-diture	-ears	-ect	-ement		
-ensurate	-eration	-et	-ge	-ger	-hting	-imum	-kage	-ked		
-lement	-lf	-mance	-me	-me	-nus	-ock	-ome	-osit	-oss	
-roll	-se	-shake	-sion	-slip	-te	-time	-tions	-tive	-ub	-ve

1.   A **wa**_____ is money that is normally paid to an employee on a weekly basis, and a **sal**_____ is money that is usually paid to an employee monthly on a regular basis.

2.   **Remun**_____ is the formal word for money that an employee receives for doing his/her job.

3.   When we work for more than the normal working time, we say that we work (and therefore earn) **over**_____.

4.   An automatic and regular increase in pay is called an **incr**_____.

5.   Money that is removed from our earnings to pay for tax, national insurance, etc, is called a **dedu**_____.

6.   If we remove money from somebody's wages (for example, because they are late), we say that we **do**_____ their wages.

7.   The **min**_____ wage is the lowest hourly wage which a company can legally pay its employees.

8.   Time for which work is paid at twice the normal rate (for example, on national holidays) is called **dou**_____ **ti**_____ .

9.   An employee who receives his/her normal rate of pay, + 50% extra (for example, by working later than normal or during unsocial hours) is said to earn **ti**_____ **and a ha**_____ .

10.   A **pen**_____ **pl**_____ helps people to save money for when they retire from work.

11.   When you want more money for the work you do, you might ask your boss for a **ri**_____ .

12.   If an employee needs some of his/her wages paid before the usual pay day, he / she might ask for an **adv**_____ (known informally as a **s**_____).

13.   A **pay**_____ shows an employee how much pay he/she has received, and how much has been removed for tax, insurance, etc.

14.   An extra payment made in addition to a normal payment (usually received by sales people for selling more than their quota) is called a **bo**_____.

15.   A **pay**_____ is the list a company keeps that shows all the people employed and paid by that company.

16.   A rewards **pac**_____ is the money and other benefits offered with a job.

For reference see *Dictionary of Business - 4th edition* (A&C Black Publishers Ltd, 978-0-713-67918-2)

17. A **weig_____** is an additional amount of money paid to an employee to compensate him/her for living in an expensive area.

18. By law, British companies have to give their employees the right to take paid holidays: this is known as **lea_____ entit_____**.

19. **Inc_____** is another word for the money that people receive for working. The money that they spend is known as **expen_____.**

20. Some companies offer their employees **st_____ op_____** , which means that the employees can buy stocks at a price lower than the normal price.

21. Some companies have **incen_____ pl_____**, where they offer their employees extra rewards and benefits for good attendance, increased productivity, etc.

22. The amount of money an employee receives each hour, day, week, etc, is known as an hourly / daily / weekly **ra_____**.

23. If an employee loses his / her job because the company doesn't need or can't afford to keep him/her, they might receive **redun_____ p_____.**

24. Some companies offer their employees a **dis_____** on the product and services they sell, which means that the employee can buy them for less than the usual price.

25. If an employee takes a job in another town or city which is a long way from his / her original home and place of work, he/she might be offered a **reloc_____ allow_____.**

26. Extra money paid to employees who work in jobs where there is a risk of personal injury is called **dan_____** money.

27. **Gr_____** is an adjective used to describe an employee's earnings before tax, national insurance, etc, have been removed.

28. **N_____** is an adjective used to describe an employee's earnings after tax, national insurance, etc, have been removed.

29. When the money that an employee receives rises automatically by the percentage increase in the cost of living, we say that it is **in_____-lin_____.**

30. When the money that an employee earns is based on age, experience, qualifications, position in the company, etc, we say that it is **comm_____.**

31. Wages are normally paid in **arr_____** , which means that they are paid at the end of the working period (for example, at the end of the week or month that the employee has worked).

32. When an employer pays an employee his/her wages directly into his/her bank account, we say that it is paid by **dir_____ dep_____** .

33. Some wages and salaries are **perfor_____ rel_____**. This means that the money that an employee receives will be based on how well he/she carries out their duties.

34. When an employee leaves his/her job after a long period with the company, he/she might be offered a large amount of money known as a **gol_____ hand_____.**

Also see *Earnings, rewards and benefits 2* on the next page

14

Complete the text with appropriate words and expressions from the box. The first one has been done for you.

acceptance bonus	attendance bonus	basic	benefits	commissions

acceptance bonus   attendance bonus   basic   benefits   commissions
comradeship   development   ~~direct~~   duvet days   extras   extrinsic   fixed
flexible   gainsharing   growth   incentive   indirect   insurance   intrinsic
motivation   pensions   performance-related   premium bonus   production bonus
profit sharing   recognition   satisfaction   security   share   skill   status

Rewards for work fall into two main groups.

The first, and in many opinions the most important, is that of **1.** _**direct**_ or **2.** _____
rewards. These are real, material rewards, and include **3.** _____ pay (a guaranteed wage or
salary paid by the hour, or on a weekly or monthly basis), and **4.** _____ pay, which is linked to
how well an employee or a group of employees works. This includes **5.** _____ - money paid
to a salesperson or group of salespeople which is usually a percentage of the sales made. Some
companies also offer **6.** _____ pay, usually given only to individual employees who work
particularly well, or who make a significant contribution to the company. **7.** _____, which is
similar to this, is extra money paid to a group or company for increased productivity, and is often
offered in order to increase **8.** _____: it is also sometimes known as a **9.** _____. If an
employee takes less than the standard time to finish a task, s/he might receive a **10.** _____.
Some employers also offer an **11.** _____ for employees who are very rarely absent from work.
If an employer is particularly keen to recruit somebody, they might offer him / her an
12. _____ when s/he agrees to join the organisation. **13.** _____, the practice of dividing
profits among the employees, is another reward which is often offered.

In addition to payment, other rewards may be offered. These include **14.** _____(known
informally as **15.** _____) such as a company car, **16.** _____, free meals, **17.**
option schemes, holidays, health **18.** _____ and **19.** _____
(a new concept, especially common in the USA, in which an employee can call their office and say
they do not feel like coming to work even though they are not ill). Benefits are usually **20.**
, which means that the employee is not able to choose what s/he gets, but some companies offer
21. _____ benefits, where the employee can choose from a menu of benefits on offer. **22.**
plans, which offer employees increased rewards and benefits for good attendance, behaviour and
productivity are becoming increasingly common.

The second group of rewards are **23.** _____ or **24.** _____. These are non-material, and
include **25.** _____ (people enjoy being in an important position or a position of authority), job
26. _____, the opportunities for personal **27.** _____, the chance to learn a new
28. _____, and career **29.** _____ opportunities. Safety and **30.** _____ at work can
also be included in this group, and for most employees, **31.** _____ (being with a group of
people you like and get on with) is also a very important reward.

For reference see *Dictionary of Business - 4th edition* (A&C Black Publishers Ltd, 978-0-713-67918-2)

Formal words

In a business / office environment, we often use 'formal' words, especially in our written English (letters, reports, contracts, etc). For example, instead of 'asked for advice', we might use 'consulted'.

We **asked** our accountant **for advice** about our tax.
becomes:
We **consulted** our accountant about our tax.

These 'formal' words are often verbs.

Exercise 1: Change the 'neutral' verbs and expressions in **bold** in sentences 1 – 15 to more 'formal' words using the verbs / expressions in the box. Each sentence requires only *one* word or expression. In most cases, you will need to change the form of the verb.

address	adjourn	adjust	administer	admonish	analyse	annul	appeal to
	appoint	assess at	assign	audit	avert	await	award

1. We need to **examine in detail** the market potential of these new products.
2. The value of the business was **calculated to be** £5 million.
3. The management increased their offer in the hope of **stopping** the strike **happening**.
4. It will be the HR manager's job to **organise** the induction programme.
5. He was **given** the job of checking the sales figures.
6. The contract was **cancelled** by the court.
7. Our accountants have been asked to **examine** the accounts for the last quarter.
8. When he was dismissed, he **asked** his union **for support**.
9. The chairman **spoke to** the sales team.
10. At the meeting it was decided to **give** middle management a salary increase.
11. Following a breach of safety procedures, the workers were **told off** by their manager.
12. We are **waiting for** the decision of the planning department.
13. Prices will be **changed** according to the current rate of inflation.
14. The chairman **stopped** the meeting until 3 o'clock.
15. We have **chosen** a new distribution manager.

advise	amalgamate	assist	assure	attempt	attend	dismiss	elect
	engage	license	present	sequester	settle	tender	waive

Exercise 2: Instructions as above.
1. The chairman has asked all managers to **come to** the meeting.
2. We have been **told** that the shipment will arrive next week.
3. Can you **help** me with these income tax returns?
4. The different unions have **joined together to make one main union**.
5. We will **try** to deliver within the next few days.
6. They have **promised** us that the delivery will be made on time.

For reference see *Dictionary of Business* - 4th edition (A&C Black Publishers Ltd, 978-0-713-67918-2)

7. The union has had its funds **taken away by order of the courts**.
8. The insurance company refused to **pay** his claim for storm damage.
9. After a lot of thought, he decided to **hand in** his resignation.
10. The court **refused to accept** his claim for compensation.
11. If we increase production, we will need to **take on** more staff.
12. He has **given up** his right to early retirement.
13. The HR director will **talk about** the new staff structure to the Board.
14. He **chose** to take early retirement.
15. The company has been **given formal permission** to sell spare parts.

Exercise 3: In this exercise, the words you need to replace those in bold are in brackets at the end of each sentence. Although they are in their correct form (e.g., the tense is correct), the letters are in the wrong order. Rearrange these letters to make words, and write them in the appropriate space in the grid below. If you do this correctly, you will reveal a word in the shaded vertical strip that can be used to replace the word in **bold** in number 13. To help you, some of the letters are in their correct space in the grid.

1. The management agreed to measures to **keep** experienced staff **in the company**. (ntreia)
2. Candidates are asked to **state clearly** which of the posts they are applying for. (fesiypc)
3. We closed the design department and **moved** the workforce **to another department**. (edeepldory)
4. We **asked** our accountant **for advice** about our tax. (tecsldonu)
5. The union has **agreed** not to call a strike without further negotiation. (duanrtnkee)
6. The union demanded that the sacked workers should be **allowed to return to the jobs from which they were dismissed**. (stindatere)
7. We are **trying to find out about** the background of the new supplier. (unnirigiq)
   (note that before '*the background*', you must also add '*into*')
8. The management **agreed** to the union's proposals. (tenscoden)
9. The management were **formally told** of the union's decision. (fotneiid)
10. The sales people were **told** about the new product **in detail**. (ierdfeb)
11. The chairman **gave a general description of** the company's plans for the coming year. (lioedtnu)
12. Her job has been **increased in importance** to senior manager level. (egupdrad)
13. The company is **sharing** production costs according to projected revenue.

1.				E				N			
2.						E				Y	
3.		R					Y				
4.				C		S					
5.		N					E				
6.			S		A						
7.			Q				G				
8.			C		S						
9.						I		E			
10.		B			F						
11.	T				D						
12.			P	R							

For reference see *Dictionary of Business - 4th edition* (A&C Black Publishers Ltd, 978-0-713-67918-2)

Business idioms

Exercise 1: Choose the correct idiomatic word or expression in (a), (b), (c) or (d), for each of these sentences.

1.   When a project goes wrong or fails, we can say that it:
      (a) puts its foot in it (b) goes belly up (c) sticks its oar in (d) gets its knickers in a twist
2.   We sometimes say that people who compete for success in business or in a career are *working for the*:
      (a) horse race   (b) dog race   (c) rat race   (d) camel race
3.   The practice of transferring a difficult, incompetent or non-essential employee from one department to another is known informally as a:
      (a) weasel waltz   (b) turkey trot   (c) cat calypso   (d) rabbit rumba
4.   We might refer to a bad employer with a reputation for losing talented staff as:
      (a) a people churner (b) a people mixer (c) a people stirrer (d) a people beater
5.   The sudden moment that you realise you have made a terrible mistake is known as:
      (a) an ohnosecond   (b) a gordonbennettminute   (c) a whoopsadaisyinstant
      (d) a hellsbellsmoment
6.   If you do a lot of different types of work in an office for very low pay, you could be referred to (unkindly) as:
      (a) a pig in a poke   (b) the cat's whiskers   (c) a a gift horse   (d) a dogsbody
7.   When an employee telephones to say that s/he is not coming to work because s/he is ill, but in fact is only *pretending* to be ill, we say that s/he is *throwing*:
      (a) the book at someone   (b) a wobbly   (c) a punch   (d) a sickie
8.   If an employee gets very angry at work because of something bad or unpleasant that happens, we can say that they are experiencing:
      (a) office anger   (b) work rage   (c) shopfloor strops   (d) workplace wobblies
9.   If an employee is deliberately or accidentally excluded from decision-making processes, they might complain that they are being left:
      (a) out of their mind   (b) out of the blue   (c) out of their head   (d) out of the loop
10.   Work that offers the same money for less effort than another similar job is often known as:
      (a) a cushy number   (b) a doddle   (c) a pushover   (d) child's play
11.   When somebody is dismissed from their job, we can say that they have:
      (a) got the shoe   (b) got the sandal   (c) got the boot   (d) got the slipper
12.   If you criticize somebody in writing, we can say that you _____ them.
      (a) pencil-smack   (b) pencil-thrash   (c) pencil-punch   (d) pencil-whip
13.   A general or broad view of a problem as a whole (which does not go into details) is known as:
      (a) a bird's-eye view   (b) a helicopter view   (c) a mountaintop view   (d) a balloon view
14.   The lazy practice of working only when a supervisor is present and able to see you is called:
      (a) lip service   (b) hand service   (c) nose service   (d) eye service
15.   If your job is unpleasant, you might say that you have:
      (a) a nose job   (b) a job lot   (c) a jobsworth   (d) a mushroom job
16.   If you consider your job to be silly, trivial and unimportant, you might describe it as:
      (a) a Tom and Jerry job (b) a Mickey Mouse job (c) a Homer Simpson job
      (d) a Donald Duck job
17.   A lazy employee who only pretends to work is said to be:
      (a) swinging the lead (b) swinging a cat (c) swinging the balance (d) swinging both ways
18.   A new product (especially a new car) that has some major defects is known as:
      (a) an orange   (b) a raspberry   (c) a melon   (d) a lemon

For reference see *Dictionary of Business* - 4*th* edition (A&C Black Publishers Ltd, 978-0-713-67918-2)

Exercise 2: Complete dialogues 1 - 16 with the most appropriate word or expression from the box. There are six words or expressions that you do not need.

basket case	bean counter	busymeet	cash cow	dead wood
dumbsizing	ear candy	empty suit	glad-hand	goldbricker
graveyard shift	happy camper	idea hamster	kiss up to	
mover and shaker	seagull manager	shape up or ship out		stress puppy
toxic employee	trim the fat	wiggle room	wombat	

1.   A. Tim seems to enjoy being under a lot of pressure, but this doesn't stop him from complaining all the time.
      B. I know, but he's not the only _____ in this company.

2.   A. I've told Tom that unless he improves his performance at work, he'll be fired.
      B. Good. It's about time somebody told him to _____.

3.   A. Tom always dresses well and follows procedure, but he doesn't actually contribute much to the company.
      B. I agree. He's a typical _____.

4.   A. The only way to get promoted in this job is to flatter and be very attentive to the senior managers.
      B. That's terrible! You shouldn't have to _____ people to get ahead in your job.

5.   A. We need to get rid of some of our older and less productive staff.
      B. I agree. The _____ has to go as soon as possible.

6.   A. Ms Rigden met a lot of people at the conference, didn't she?
      B. She certainly did. I think I saw her _____ almost everyone there.

7.   A. The company brought in a so-called expert to deal with a big project, but he just made a lot of fuss, achieved absolutely nothing and then left.
      B. Well, he wasn't the first _____ we've had, and I'm sure he won't be the last.

8.   A. My boss always tells me how well I'm doing, but he never offers me a pay rise.
      B. Well, I suppose a bit of _____ is better than nothing.

9.   A. I can't believe we sat in that meeting and listened to the boss talk for over three hours.
      B. Me neither. What a complete _____!

10.   A. We need to reduce the size of the company but we need to make sure it doesn't become unprofitable or inefficient.
      B. That's true. _____ is something we need to avoid at all costs.

11.   A. Do you enjoy your work here?
      B. Oh, absolutely. I'm a regular _____.

12.   A. We're expected to sign the contract by tomorrow.
      B. That's no good. We only received it yesterday. We need a bit of _____.

13.   A. Have you seen Alan today?
      B. He's in a _____ all morning. He should be free at lunchtime.

14.   A. Is the company doing well?
      B. No, not at all. As far as I'm concerned, it's a complete _____!

15.   A. Business is dropping off and we could end up in financial trouble.
      B. I know. Perhaps it's time to _____.

16.   A. Do you think there will be a lot of demand for our latest range of T-shirts?
      B. Oh absolutely. It's a _____. Everyone will want one!

For reference see *Dictionary of Business - 4th edition* (A&C Black Publishers Ltd, 978-0-713-67918-2)

IT and e-commerce

Exercise 1: Read this (not very technical) description and replace the underlined expressions with a more appropriate word or expression from the box.

anti-virus software   attachment   bookmark   browser   CD / DVD drive
chatrooms   components   CPU (central processing unit)   crashing   delete
desktop   domain (name)   download   DTP (desktop publishing)   email
hard disk   hard drive   homepage   Internet   keyboard   keywords   laptop
links   load   log on   log out   memory   memory stick   monitor   mouse
newsgroups   on-line   password   pop-up   printer   scanner   provider
search engine   software   Spam®   spreadsheets   update   USB port
virus   website   word processing

This is my new **1.** computer that sits on top of a table or desk (I've also got a **2.** small computer which can be carried and held on your knees.) As you can see, there are six main **3.** parts to it. The first is the **4.** part of the computer that runs it and controls what it does, and this is the most important bit. It carries the **5.** part that stores and controls the flow of information, including the **6.** round thing that is used for storing information. Mine has a particularly high **7.** capacity for storing information, which means that it's much faster than most. It came with its own **8.** computer programs package (including one for **9.** writing, checking and changing texts, one for **10.** calculating in columns of figures, and one for **11.** producing texts and pictures for magazines). You can also **12.** put in other programs using the **13.** sliding tray for carrying round, plastic, information-holding things, or the **14.** hole for connecting computer parts to one another (into which you can put a **15.** small plastic and metal object which can hold a lot of information).

The other five parts of the computer are the **16.** screen that lets you see what your computer is doing, the **17.** flat thing with the letters and numbers on it that let you control the computer, the **18.** machine that lets you make copies of the documents that you create on your computer, the **19.** device for making colour copies of photographs and other documents which you can put onto your computer and last but not least, the **20.** device that you hold in your hand and move across your desk to control the cursor.

In my opinion, the best thing about modern information technology is the **21.** network that links millions of computers from around the world. Once you've got yourself a **22.** company that allows you access and a **23.** program that finds information you can start using this. It's especially useful if you want to get information about something, go shopping or **24.** transfer information, games, music, etc, onto your own computer. You can even 'talk' to other computer users in **25.** special places where you can leave messages and get instant replies. If you have a particular interest in something, you can also visit **26.** places on the computer where you can 'talk' to other people with the same interest.

Most companies have their own **27.** special computer pages which you can look at. Let me **28.** turn the computer on, enter my code and access the computer system, and I'll show you ours. OK, here we go. Oh no, another **29.** advertisement that suddenly appears on the computer screen. How annoying. Let me just remove it. That's better.

For reference see *Dictionary of Business - 4th edition* (A&C Black Publishers Ltd, 978-0-713-67918-2)

Now, I can never remember the exact address of our company, so first of all I'll type it into the **30.** program that helps you find the information you want. OK, *A and C Black Publishing*'. The computer identifies the **31.** most important or main words and then gives me **32.** connections to a list of possible sites. This one looks right: 'www.acblack.com'. That's the company's **33.** officially registered website address. I'll click on that.

Bingo! Here's our **34.** front page. You can use this to find the different books that we publish, and if you want you can even buy them **35.** through the computer. Hmm, this book looks good: '*Check your English Vocabulary for Business and Administration*'. Now, before I **36.** exit this site, I'll just **37.** add it to my list of favourites so that I can find it more quickly next time.

Perhaps the most important thing, however, is **38.** a special electronic letter-sending facility, which allows you to communicate with people around the world in an instant. Let me quickly check mine. First of all, I need to enter my **39.** special word that allows me to enter the system. That's it. Oh dear, nothing very interesting. Mainly a load of **40.** unwanted advertising. I'll just **41.** remove it: I don't particularly want to have a new home extension, pass my bank details to a "solicitor" in Nigeria or buy a pill that's guaranteed to improve my love life.

There's something here from one of our suppliers with a / an **42.** document or file that has been sent with it. You have to be careful with these: sometimes they contain a **43.** hidden routine placed in the program that destroys or corrupts files. If you open it, it can do all sorts of horrible things to your computer. We had one last week that kept **44.** shutting down our system. We do have **45.** something on our computer that protects against this sort of thing, but it's a bit out of date: we really ought to **46.** bring it up to date.

Exercise 2: Test your knowledge with this quiz.

1. What is a *JPEG* and what would you use it for?
2. In computer terms, what is the difference between a *file* and a *folder*?
3. What is the difference between *freeware* and *shareware*?
4. You suspect that *spyware* is being used on your computer each time you use the Internet. What does this do?
5. What is the difference between the *Internet*, an *intranet* and an *extranet*?
6. A customer using your website to buy something has just checked her *shopping basket* and is now *proceeding to checkout*. What is she about to do?
7. What is a *click-wrap agreement*? Is it:
    (a) a contract presented entirely over the Internet
    (b) an agreement between two or more companies to share a single website
    (c) an agreement between two or more companies to pass customer information to each other
    (d) a contract that is sent over the Internet and then returned in the normal post
    (e) an agreement by a company not to send unsolicited advertising to customers.
8. What do the letters *ISP* stand for?
9. What do we call information that a website leaves in your computer so that the website recognises you when you visit it again? Is it:
    (a) a biscuit **(b)** a cookie **(c)** a cracker **(d)** a scone **(e)** a crumpet

For reference see *Dictionary of Business - 4th edition* (A&C Black Publishers Ltd, 978-0-713-67918-2)

10. The company you work for sells its products on the Internet, and also in its own shops around the country. What is the name we give to this kind of operation? Is it:

    (a) a mouse and house business   **(b)** a tap and trot business   **(c)** a clicks and mortar business   **(d)** a hit and run business   **(e)** a surf and turf business

11. Many company websites have a section or page labelled *FAQ*. What do these letters stand for?

12. An on-line shop has a small padlock symbol (🔒) displayed at the bottom of the computer screen. What does this mean?:

    (a) The website or webpage has a secure server.
    (b) The website will not allow the user to proceed any further.
    (c) The Internet connection has been broken.
    (d) There is, or may be, a virus on the site.
    (e) The user needs to enter a password to continue.

13. Your company does a lot of *B2B* advertising on the Internet. What does this mean?

14. You send an email, and then almost immediately receive a message saying that the person you are trying to contact is on holiday. What do we call this sort of message?

15. UCE is the official term for:

    (a) an on-line shop that only sells on the Internet   **(b)** spam   **(c)** a username or password   **(d)** a dotcom enterprise   **(e)** a domain name

16. What is *broadband*? Is this the same as an *ISDN line*?

17. You are *uploading* information on your computer. Are you:

    (a) transferring information from the Internet or another application to your computer?
    (b) transferring information from your computer to a website?

18. Some websites (especially those belonging to on-line banks) ask their customers for a *PIN* before they can enter the site. What do these letters stand for?

19. In an IT context, what are *banners*, *buttons* and *pop-ups*?

20. You discover that there is an *anti-site* on the Internet dedicated to your company. Would you be happy about this?

21. What does a computer *hacker* do?

22. In an IT context, what does a *firewall* do?

23. Your company has just been *Amazoned*. What has happened to it?

24. Someone tells you that your company has a *sticky site*. What do they mean?

    (a) Your company website is very slow.
    (b) The information on your company website is out of date.
    (c) Your company website is very boring.
    (d) Your company website is very difficult to use.
    (e) Your company website is very interesting.

25. Someone accuses your company of *phishing*. What do they think you have done?

26. A customer says you have a *cobweb site* that looks like an *angry fruit salad*. How would you feel about this?

27. Your company website has a lot of *spider food*. From a business point of view, why might this be an advantage to you?

28. Are you *buzzword compliant*?

For reference see *Dictionary of Business - 4th edition* (A&C Black Publishers Ltd, 978-0-713-67918-2)

Exercise 1: Look at the list of different jobs in the box, and match each one with the person who is speaking in 1 – 15.

Assistant Manager   Chairman   Chief Executive Officer (CEO)   Company Director   Company Secretary   Girl Friday   Human Resources (HR)   Manager   Managing Director (MD)   Non-executive Director   Personal Assistant (PA)   Production Manager   Receptionist   Secretary   Technical Support Consultant   Trainer

1.   Hello. Welcome to Wy-T Computers. Have you got an appointment? Good. Take a seat and I'll call up to her office. Would you like a coffee while you wait?

2.   Good morning. My name is Angela Ranscombe, and I am responsible for my company's productive use of its workforce

3.   Hello. I'm Hilary Hannah. I type letters, file documents, arrange meetings and so on, for the various people in my office.

4.   Hi. My name's Sue Smith. I do a lot of small jobs in and around the office. If you want some filing done, some mail posted, or if you just want a cup of tea, I'm the one to ask!

5.   Hello. My name's Adam Dent. I help customers who are having problems with our products. I spend most of my day on the phone.

6.   I'm Anne Langsdale, and I've been appointed by the shareholders to help run the company.

7.   Hello there. Don Brown. Nice to meet you. I make sure that the company is being run efficiently and effectively.

8.   My name's Liz Hamley, and I suppose I'm the big cheese around here. Basically I'm the most important director in charge of the company.

9.   I'm Judy Briers. I work directly for Liz Hamley, and for her alone. I perform various secretarial and administrative duties for her.

10.   I'm Laurence Woodham. I'm a senior employee here, with director status and administrative and legal authority. This is a legal requirement for all limited companies in the UK.

11.   Good morning. I'm Peter Feltham, and I preside over the company's board meetings.

12.   And I'm Helen Brown. I attend board meetings, but only to listen and give advice. I cannot usually make decisions on behalf of the company.

13.   Hi there. My name's Mark Searle, and I supervise the production process.

14.   And I'm Bob Wheatley. I help Mark Searle.

15.   My name's Ryan Briggs. I'm responsible for developing our employees' potential through courses and other staff development programmes.

For reference see *Dictionary of Business - 4th edition* (A&C Black Publishers Ltd, 978-0-713-67918-2)

Exercise 2: Instructions as above.

| Accountant   Advertising Manager   Arbitrator   Area / Regional Manager
External Auditor   Foreman   Graduate Trainee   IT Consultant
Marketing Manager   Official Mediator   Official Receiver   Sales Representative
Security Guard   Telesales Manager   Trade Union Representative |

1. Good morning. I'm Edward Saville. I control the company finances. Can't stop to talk: I need to get these tax forms completed.

2. I'm Don Prescott. I've been hired by the company's head office to check Mr Saville's figures. We're not sure that everything adds up.

3. My name's Mary Myers. I actually work in the company's other office in Birmingham, and am responsible for the company's operations there.

4. I'm Sarah Keats. I'm responsible for planning and controlling our marketing activities and budgets.

5. I'm Richard Giddings. It's my job to make sure consumers know all about our latest range of products.

6. Hello. I'm Bill Kennedy. I visit clients around the country and talk to them directly about our products.

7. Morning. Barry Ramp. I'm highly skilled, I'm told, so I've been put in charge of all the workers on the factory floor.

8. Andy Kelly. Hi. I'm just an ordinary worker on the factory floor, but I represent the workers in discussions with the managers about things like wages and conditions of employment.

9. My name's Jennie Bryant. I don't actually work for the company, but there's currently a dispute going on between the workers and the management regarding pay, so I've been brought in to try to sort things out.

10. I'm Joy Bell. I don't work for the company either, but I might be officially appointed to sort out the dispute mentioned above, and make a binding decision. This will only happen if Jennie Bryant is unable to resolve it.

11. Hello. I'm Tabitha Sutcliffe. I finished university last month, and I'm here to learn a bit about the company and how it operates. I'm hoping that they'll offer me a job.

12. I'm Sam Michaud. Has your hard-drive crashed? Is your printer jammed? Can't get on line? Don't worry, I'll get it sorted out.

13. Hi. I'm Naomi Yarnton. I'm in charge of the team who contact potential clients on the phone.

14. I'm Tony Preston. Don't tell anyone here, but the company's in a lot of trouble. I'm about to take it over, sell its assets and use the proceeds to pay off all the creditors.

15. My name's Eddie Jobsworth. Have you got ID? Sorry, can't let you go any further here without ID. You're going to have to leave. Now, please.

Look at the jobs and positions in the boxes in Exercises 1 and 2 again. *Without* referring back to the sentences, try to explain in your own words what each job involves.

For reference see *Dictionary of Business - 4th edition* (A&C Black Publishers Ltd, 978-0-713-67918-2)

On the next three pages you will see extracts from 11 different types of letter. Look at each extract carefully, then match it with one of the letter types from the list in the box below. Underline the key words or phrases which helped you to decide. Each type of letter can be matched with 5 extracts, and the sentences for each letter are in the same order as they would appear in real letters. There are 5 extracts that do not match any of the letter types.

(A) Letter of introduction / application   (B) Letter of apology   (C) Invitation to interview
(D) Letter of reference   (E) Letter of rejection   (F) Letter of appointment
(G) Written warning   (H) Letter of dismissal   (I) Letter of resignation
(J) Acknowledgement of resignation   (K) Letter of complaint

1. Following the disciplinary interview which you attended on 12 June, I am writing to confirm the decision taken that you will be given a written reprimand under our Disciplinary Procedure.

2. Following your interview and our conversation yesterday, this letter is to confirm your post as Production Manager commencing 2 October.

3. Thank you for your application for the post of Production Manager at Graffix plc.

4. On 7 May, following persistent neglect of duties on your part, you were given a written warning in accordance with the Company's Disciplinary Procedure.

5. Thank you for your letter of 2 October detailing your recent unpleasant incident in our Witney branch.

6. I would like to apply for the post of Customer Relations Manager advertised in yesterday's Guardian.

7. I have known Jan Kelly since she started working with the company in 1999.

8. This will be placed in your personal record file, but will be disregarded for disciplinary purposes after a period of six months, provided your conduct reaches a satisfactory level.

9. This letter and the attached terms and conditions form the basis of your contract of employment.

10. As I told you yesterday, I have decided to hand in my notice, and this letter is to inform you of my decision to leave the company.

11. Thank you for your letter of 19 October telling us of your intention to leave the company.

12. In a letter of 18 June, you were advised that unless your conduct improved, you would be dismissed from your post.

13. Thank you for attending our interview sessions last week.

14. We are naturally most sorry that you should be leaving us, but I understand your reasons for doing so.

15. I am writing to express my dissatisfaction with the delay in your delivery of some products we ordered last month.

16. She came to work for this company as a Trainee in the production department, and rapidly moved up the scale to become Deputy Production Manager three years ago.

For reference see *Dictionary of Business - 4th edition* (A&C Black Publishers Ltd, 978-0-713-67918-2)

17. We would like you to come for a preliminary interview with our Production Director, James Mills.

18. As you can see from the attached printout of the order form, we placed this order via your website 2 weeks ago, on 13 January.

19. We notice from our records that Invoice SB/1097 has not been paid, and we would be grateful if you could settle it within 7 days.

20. I would like to reserve a single room (preferably on an upper floor) from 23 – 31 May inclusive.

21. We have spoken to the member of staff in question, and he has assured us that he was acting in accordance with company policy.

22. I am currently working as a customer care assistant for Pants2U, one of the country's biggest Internet suppliers of men's clothing, where I deal primarily with on-line customer queries.

23. I am delighted that you will be coming to work for us.

24. The notice period indicated in my contract of employment is six weeks, but you agreed during our conversation that in my case this could be reduced to four.

25. The nature of the unsatisfactory conduct was your continual lateness, persistent absenteeism, and neglect of duties on the shop floor.

26. We expect to see an improvement in your punctuality and attendance, and a more professional approach to your work by 30 June.

27. At the disciplinary hearing held on 16 October, it was decided that your performance was still unsatisfactory, and you had shown no inclination to improve.

28. Your terms and conditions clearly state that orders are processed, packed and sent on the same day, but so far we have received nothing.

29. I am sure you will find a very pleasant working environment here, and we look forward to welcoming you as a member of our team on 2 October.

30. The company you are joining has an excellent reputation, and I am sure you will be as happy there as you have been with us.

31. We would be grateful if you could send us a copy of your current catalogue and price list.

32. As I explained to you, I have been very happy working here, and shall be leaving with many regrets.

33. Unfortunately, on this occasion, I regret to tell you that your application has been unsuccessful.

34. These will be held at our Banbury office on 29 and 30 August, and should last about 30 minutes.

35. However, we take customer complaints very seriously, and I can assure you that we will look into this matter further.

36. I have however been offered a post at a substantially higher salary with another company.

37. She is a very able manager, and is particularly keen on keeping up to date with new technology.

38. You are clearly very well-motivated and have some excellent ideas, but the panel felt that overall you lacked sufficient experience.

For reference see *Dictionary of Business - 4th edition* (A&C Black Publishers Ltd, 978-0-713-67918-2)

39. I have forwarded your letter to our head office, and I will keep you informed as to any action that will be taken.

40. On behalf of Rosewain Ltd, I would like to apologise most sincerely, and hope that your experience does not put you off using our stores.

41. I would be grateful if you could call me to arrange a suitable time on one of those days.

42. I am therefore writing to confirm the decision that you will be dismissed, and that your last day of service with the company will be 2 November.

43. She has always worked well with other members of staff, has always been on time and has rarely missed work through illness.

44. This is in spite of several phone calls and emails to your office, and in spite of your repeated promises of immediate action.

45. I have noted that your last day of service with us will be 23 November, and I have passed this information to the HR Department to deal with.

46. However, I am now looking for a position with more responsibility, and one which allows me to work with customers face to face.

47. As requested, I enclose a recent CV outlining my qualifications and experience.

48. On behalf of NX Operations, I would like to wish you all the best in your search for a suitable position.

49. We will be sorry to see her leave, but I know that she is looking for a more challenging position.

50. Thank you for your letter of 15 April. We are pleased to enclose this year's catalogue and our current price list.

51. Thank you once again for the interest you have shown in our company.

52. If you have any special needs, especially concerning access, please let me know in advance.

53. Therefore, unless the goods are with us within 48 hours, we will have no option but to cancel our order and look elsewhere.

54. You have the right to appeal against this decision to the Production Director within seven days of receiving this letter of dismissal, in writing, giving your reasons.

55. Furthermore, as the prospects of further advancement are greater, I felt that this was an offer I felt I simply could not turn down.

56. If you would like any more information regarding my current position, or previous experience, please do not hesitate to contact me.

57. From your website brochure, please supply the following items: 10x8756/Ba and 15x9444/Aa. Please deliver with an invoice in triplicate to the following address:

58. On a personal level, I shall be particularly sorry to see you go; you have been an excellent manager, and I hope you will keep in touch.

59. In the meantime, if you have any queries about your new post, please do not hesitate to call me on extension 2340.

60. The likely consequence of insufficient improvement is dismissal.

For reference see *Dictionary of Business - 4th edition* (A&C Black Publishers Ltd, 978-0-713-67918-2)

Meetings and presentations

Look at this rather long-winded opening address from a company's Annual General Meeting (AGM) and fill in the gaps with words from the box. The *first* letter of each word is already in the text.

-articipants	-atters	-bjectives	-chedule	-chieve	-ddress
-ecommendations	-elcoming	-elegates	-enue	-eport	-et through	-genda
-hair	-inutes	-iscuss	-larification	-loor	-loses	-mplement	-nterrupt
-oals	-oints	-omplaints	-onference	-ontingency	-ontribute	-otes
-peakers	-pen	-pen-floor	-pinions	-resentations	-ringing up	-riority
-rogress	-ssues	-ttendance	-uestions	-ummarizing	-upporting

I'd like to **1. o**_____ this meeting by **2. w**_____ you all. It's good to see so many **3. p**_____here today - in fact, this is probably the best **4. a**_____ we've had at a meeting for a long time - and I'd like to thank you all in advance for **5. s**_____ me.

Well, we've got a lot on the **6. a**_____ and I want to make as much **7. p**_____ as possible in the next two hours or so. If we stick to the main **8. s**_____, we should **9. g**_____ everything and **10. a**_____ all of our **11. g**_____ and **12. o**_____. I will **13. c**_____ the meeting, as usual, but I really hope that you will all have something to **14. c**_____, and if anything needs **15. c**_____, please don't hesitate to **16. i**_____ me (although not too often, I hope: the more **17. i**_____ we can **18. a**_____ today the better).

I'll be **19. b**_____ several important **20. m**_____ during the meeting, beginning with those that I feel should take **21. p**_____, before **22. s**_____ the main **23. p**_____and making **24. r**_____. This will be followed by an **25. o**_____ session where you can give me your **26. o**_____. And I'm sure you will all be delighted to hear that after the meeting **27. c**_____, there will be drinks and snacks for everyone.

Mr Barker will be taking **28. n**_____ and keeping the **29. m**_____ of the meeting, and I will be using these to write my **30. r**_____ afterwards, so if anyone has any **31. c**_____, I suggest you talk to him and not to me!

Now, before I get going, are there any **32. q**_____ from the **33. f**_____? No? Good. Right, well I'll begin.

The first point I want to **34. d**_____ is next month's **35. c**_____. As you know, the **36. v**_____ we have chosen is the Royal Eynsham Hotel in Oxfordshire. We've invited several **37. s**_____ to make **38. p**_____ on various aspects of the trade, and we're expecting over 200 **39. d**_____ from our offices around Europe. Now, of course, there's always the possibility that some major players* won't be able to make it, so we need to make a **40. c**_____ plan that we can **41. i**_____ if things go pear-shaped**...

(**major players*: important people. **Pear shaped*: if something goes *pear-shaped*, it goes wrong. This is an informal expression)

For reference see *Dictionary of Business - 4th edition* (A&C Black Publishers Ltd, 978-0-713-67918-2)

Num...

How do you say the numbers and symbols in **bold** in these se...

1. **2006** was the company's most profitable year since **1994**.

2. The advantage of Internet banking is that you can check your a...

3. Despite a rigorous advertising campaign, demand has only risen... months.

4. We're meeting in his office at **3.45** this afternoon.

5. Your flight for Zurich leaves at **1800** from Gatwick South Termi...

6. I expect to be back in the country on **30 June**.

7. Our next range of products will be released on **10/3/07**.

8. She completed the test in a record **27½** minutes.

9. **¾** of all our employees think the canteen food could be impro...

10. The new desk measures exactly **2m x 1m x 1m.**

11. Is this printer really only **£10.99**?

12. Oh, sorry sir, that's a mistake. The sticker should say **£100.99.**

13. And that computer doesn't cost **£120.75**. It actually costs **£112**...

14. Please quote reference **ACB81 - 25/B.**

15. Our new telephone number is **020 7921 3567**.

16. For more information, call **0845 601 5884**.

17. Alternatively, ring **0800 231415**.

18. The emergency telephone number in the UK is **999**. In the USA...

19. To access the information you require, press the **#** key, followe... finally the ***** key.

20. He earns a salary of over **£200K** a year! In fact, he's making so... plans to retire in his **mid-50's**.

21. We have invested over **$6M** in new technology.

22. To get here from Croydon, take the **M25** northbound, then tak... westbound, leave at junction 9 and take the **A329** towards Wo...

23. The Union held a ballot to see if the workers wanted to strike... favour.

24. My email address is markbarrington**@snailmail.co.uk**.

25. Hi Todd. **GR8** news on the promotion. I'm really **:-)** for you! **CU**... drink?

26. He drives to work in a big, fuel-guzzling **4x4**.

27. Liverpool won the match against Arsenal by **2:0**. In the match... United the following week, they drew **3:3**.

28. At the last census, the population of the country was **37,762,4**...

29. This book is **©** Rawdon Wyatt, 2007.

30. The 'Ultimafone**®**' has just won a 'Product of the Year' award.

Money and financial issues

Exercise 1: Complete these definitions with words or expressions from the box. In each case, the words / expressions you need are connected in some way: for example, they might have a similar meaning, they might be related to the same business issue, or they might be opposites (but often used together when talking about the same topic). You will need to use one word from the box twice.

audit	balance	bankrupt	borrow	budget	commission	compound	credit
debit	default	deflation	deposit	discount	dividend	duty	exorbitant
expenditure	fund	gross	honour	income	inflation	insolvent	interest
invoice	lend	net	overpriced	pension	rebate	receipt	redundancy pay
refund	royalty	salary	shares	simple	sponsor	statement	stocks	subsidize
tax	underwrite	venture capital	wage	withdraw	working capital

1. If you _____ money to someone, you let someone use your money for a certain period of time. If you _____ money from someone, you take someone's money for a short time (usually paying *interest* and then *repaying* it).

2. When you _____ an account, you put money into it. When you _____ an account, you take money out of it.

3. If a company is _____, it has lost all its money. If a company is _____, it has lost all its money, it has also borrowed a lot, and it cannot pay back its *debts* (= money it owes).

4. A _____ is part of a company's profits shared out among shareholders (see number 18). A _____ is money paid to the author of a book, an actor, a rock star, etc, as a percentage of sales.

5. In the UK, _____ are one of the many equal parts into which a public company's capital is divided. _____ are similar, but are issued by the government.

6. _____ profit is the profit you make *before* money is taken away to cover costs of production, labour, tax, etc. _____ profit is the money you are left with *after* costs, taxes, etc, have been taken away (money which is taken away is called a *deduction*).

7. If you _____ money in an account, you put money into the account. If you _____ money, you take it out of your account.

8. _____ is money taken by the government from incomes, sales, etc, to pay for government services. _____ is money that has to be paid for bringing goods into a country.

9. _____ is the money you receive (for example, your *wage* or *salary*). _____ is money you spend.

10. Something which is _____ is too expensive. Something which is _____ costs much more than its true value.

11. A _____ is money that is earned on a daily or weekly basis (often for a part-time, temporary or unskilled job). A _____ is money that is earned monthly or annually (usually for a full-time, permanent or skilled job or profession).

12. An _____ is a note, or *bill*, sent to you to ask for payment for goods or services. A _____ is a note (from a shop, for example) which shows how much you have paid for something.

13. A _____ is the percentage by which a full price is reduced in a shop. A _____ is money paid back to a customer when, for example, returning something to a shop.

14. A _____ is money paid back to a customer when, for example, returning something to a shop (see number 13 above). A _____ is money that someone gets back as a result of paying too much tax or rent, etc.

15. _____ is a state of economy where prices and wages in_
of economic activity (usually accompanied by a drop in pric_

16. A _____ is the money that someone continues to receiv_
_____ is the money that is given to someone to compe_
company no longer needs them and has to dismiss them.

17. A bank _____ is a detailed written document from a ba_
into and come out of a bank account. A _____ is the an_
account.

18. _____ is the percentage of sales value given to a sales p_
percentage that is paid to someone for lending money.

19. _____ interest is interest calculated on the sum of the o_
interest. _____ interest is interest that is calculated on th_
not include the interest already earned.

20. _____ is the money that is needed or available for runni_
_____ is the money that is needed or available for starti_

21. If you _____ a plan or venture, you provide the money f_
you provide the money for it, and also assume financial res_

22. An _____ is an official examination of the financial reco_
A _____ is the amount of money a company, organisati_
something.

23. If you _____ goods or services, you pay part of the cost_
lower price. If you _____ something (for example, an ev_

24. If you _____ a debt, you pay back the money you owe._
the money back.

Exercise 2: Here are 30 two- and three-word expressio_
finance issues. In either the first, second or third wor_
removed. Replace the letters in each case. Use a diction_
expression.

1. Business   o_e_h_a_s
2. C_e_i__ risk
3. P_n_i_n plan
4. Profit m_r_i__
5. E_c_a_g_ rate
6. C_s__ flow
7. Credit l_m_t
8. C_p_t_l gains
9. Down p_y_e_t
10. R_s_ management
11. Money _a_n_e_i_g
12. Offshore b_n_i_g
13. Foreign __u_r_n_y
14. V_l_e added tax
15. Net __p_r_t_n__ income

16. Operating __r_f_
17. Interest r_t_
18. B_d_e_a_y c_
19. F_n_n_e comp_
20. Expense __c_o_
21. Return on i_v_
22. Rate of r_t_r_
23. Real a_s_t_
24. D_n_m_c pric_
25. Management b_
26. Budget d_f_c_
27. C_n_u_e_ sp_
28. I_c_m_ tax
29. G_l_e_ handsl_
30. Price __n_e_s_

Also see *Earnings, rewards and benefits* on pages 13-15_

Phrasal verbs 1

Complete the sentences below with a verb from the left-hand box, and a particle from the right-hand box, to make *phrasal verbs*. The meaning of each phrasal verb is explained in brackets at the end of each sentence. Write your answers in the crossword grid on the third page (you will not need to put a gap between the verb and the particle). The first one has been done as an example.

Note that you will need to use some of the verbs and particles more than once, and in some cases you will need to change their form (for example, to past simple). Also note that in some cases, more than one answer may be possible, but only one will fit into the crossword grid.

Verbs
back   break   bring   build   burn   call cancel   carry   cut   fall   fight   fill   find gear   get   give   hand   hold   opt   phase put   run   stand   take   turn

Particles
across   against   ahead   back behind   down   in   into   off on   out   over   up   with

(⇨ = across in the crossword grid, ⇩ = down)

1⇩   Your suggestions sound good. Let's **_run_** **_with_** them for a while. (*informal: to decide to carry out an idea or project*)

2⇨   The unions are _____ _____ the proposed redundancies. (*to struggle to try to overcome something*)

3⇩   The manager tried to _____ _____ to the workforce the reasons why some people were being made redundant. (*to make someone understand something*)

4⇨   He _____ _____ the job he was offered. (*to refuse something, such as an offer of help*)

5⇨   There isn't enough work, so we have to _____ some of you _____ for the day. (*to reduce employee's hours of work because of shortage of work*)

6⇩   We don't know if they will agree to our terms, and we won't _____ _____ until next week. (*to discover a fact or piece of information*)

7⇨   The workers refused to _____ _____ any of their rights. (*to hand something to someone, or to lose something, often as the result of pressure from someone*)

8⇩   The new system of pension contributions will be _____ _____ over the next two months. (*to introduce / bring something in gradually*)

9⇨   We expect negotiations to _____ _____ into the night. (*to continue*)

10⇨   If she decides to take early retirement, she'll probably _____ _____ her responsibilities to her deputy. (*to pass your work responsibilities to someone else*)

11⇩   The management have refused to _____ _____ to pressure from the unions. (*to yield or to surrender*)

12⇨   After an agreement was reached, the union _____ _____ the strike. (*to stop a planned course of action or an event*)

13⇩   Mr Smith is currently _____ _____ for the chairman, who is ill. (*to take someone's place*)

14⇩   Despite serious personal problems, he has _____ _____ the same job for the last six years. (*to manage to do a difficult job, usually over a long period of time*)

15⇨   You must _____ all the forecasts _____ the budget. (*to add something to something else that is being set up*)

16⇩ The company was _____ _____ and separate divisions sold off. (*to split something large into small sections*)

17⇨ We may decide to _____ _____ the price of some of our brands to help increase demand. (*to reduce*)

17⇩ We plan to _____ _____ a new model of the car for the motor show. (*to produce something new*)

18⇨ Payment will be _____ _____ until the contract has been signed. (*to wait, to not go forward*)

19⇨ Make sure you don't make any mistakes when you _____ _____ the application form. (*to write the required information in the spaces on a form*)

20⇨ Negotiations between management and the unions _____ _____ after six hours. (*to stop a negotiation, usually because no agreement has been made*)

20⇩ At the meeting, the chairman _____ _____ the subject of redundancy payments. (*to refer to something for the first time*)

21⇨ The company is _____ itself _____ for expansion into the African market. (*informal: to get ready*)

22⇩ We have installed networked computers to _____ _____ on paperwork. (*to reduce the amount of something used*)

23⇨ Don't work too hard or you'll _____ yourself _____ (*informal: to become tired and incapable of further work because of stress*)

24⇩ We had to cancel the project when our German partners _____ _____. (*to stop being a part of a deal or arrangement*)

25⇩ After several years with the company, she _____ _____ a new post with one of our competitors. (*to start a new job*)

26⇩ The contract signing was _____ _____ because of disagreements over some of the terms and conditions. (*to delay*)

27⇨ He _____ _____ well in his new job, and was soon promoted. (*to succeed*)

28⇩ It's very important to _____ _____ your duties to the best of your ability. (*to do what is necessary for your job*)

29⇩ If you complain, you might _____ your money _____. (*to receive something which you had before*)

30⇩ The accounts department _____ _____ the draft accounts in time for the meeting. (*to produce something*)

31⇨ If you want to _____ _____ in your job, you'll need to show more commitment. (*to advance in your career*)

32⇨ The meeting has been _____ _____ for two weeks. (*to arrange for something to take place later than planned*)

33⇨ We are planning to _____ _____ most of our work to freelancers. (*to send or give a job to someone else, usually not in your company*)

34⇨ Do you think they'll _____ _____ when they realise how hard the project is? (*to decide not to do something*)

35⇩ Have the managers agreed to _____ _____ more staff for the Witney office? (*to employ*)

36⇨ Higher costs have _____ _____ the increased sales revenue. (*to balance or act against each other and so make each other invalid*)

37⇨ In the last six months we have _____ _____ our rivals. (*to have fewer sales or make less profit than another company*)

33

For reference see *Dictionary of Business - 4th edition* (A&C Black Publishers Ltd, 978-0-713-67918-2)

Match the questions on the left with the most appropriate answers on the right. The answers contain a definition or an explanation of the phrasal verbs in **bold** on the left.

1. Would you **advise against** moving the head office to Edinburgh?

2. Did you manage to **turn** the company **round**?

3. Do you think the staff will **walk out** when they hear the news?

4. Did you manage to **get through to** the complaints department?

5. Shall we **put back** the meeting until everyone can come?

6. Were the management willing to **improve on** their previous offer?

7. Would the staff be prepared to **hold out for** a 10% pay rise?

8. Will we be able to **hold** him **to** the contract?

9. Can we **clock off** yet?

10. Have you **taken over** the company?

11. Are they hoping to **build up** a profitable business?

12. Did you **sort out** the accounts problem with the auditor?

13. Have our reps **called in** to give us their sales figures.

14. Can we pay you half now, and **make up** the difference next month?

15. Can we **get along** all right with only half the staff we had before?

16. Do you think the company will **close down** its branch in Banbury?

17. Are you worried that our partners will **go back on** their agreement?

18. Did you get my notice? I **handed** it **in** on Tuesday.

19. Can you **follow up** our proposal as soon as possible?

20. Do you think it's time that AZ Products were **phased out** as a supplier of spare parts?

A. Yes, they thought they might be able to do a bit better as long as we were prepared to work harder.

B. Possibly. We'll stop using them gradually while we start using other sources.

C. Well, we haven't actually bought it yet, but we've made an offer to buy most of the shares.

D. No, we didn't receive anything in writing.

E. Possibly. It won't be the first time they've not done something that they've promised.

F. Yes, I don't think we should do that for the time being.

G. Well, another £60 a week is an improvement, I suppose, but they won't want to wait too long.

H. Yes, I've had three phone calls already this afternoon.

I. Fine. Credit us with the outstanding balance on your next statement.

J. Well, there has already been some gradual expansion, but it's going to take time.

K. Of course. We'll be examining it in detail at the next meeting.

L. Well, I certainly think it's a good idea to move it to a later date.

M. Yes, it was making a loss, but now it's a very profitable organisation.

N. I hope so. We've been promised that the terms we've set out will be honoured.

O. I don't know, but if they do, that's the third one they'll have shut this year.

P. We should manage, although everyone will have to work a bit harder.

Q. Yes, it's time to leave. Let's go home.

R. Probably, but we really don't want everyone to stop working and leave in protest.

S. Yes. Everything has been put in order at last.

T. No, they weren't answering the phone.

For reference see *Dictionary of Business - 4th edition* (A&C Black Publishers Ltd, 978-0-713-67918-2)

Production and operations

Exercise 1: Complete each sentence 1 – 15 with two words to make an expression connected with production and operations. The first word should come from the left-hand box, and the second word should come from the right-hand box. Each sentence is followed by a definition of the expression you need. Use each word once only.

assembly capacity finished lead manufacturing offshore optimum planned product purchasing random raw resource supply zero

allocation capacity chain costs defects goods line materials obsolescence planning power production recall sampling time

1. Unless our supplier reduces its _____ _____ , we will have to radically change the way we operate. (*the length of time that lapses between placing an order for something and receiving it*)

2. The recession has led to a drop in overall _____ _____ , which means that we will have to reduce output on some of our less popular lines. (*the quantity of goods or services which can be bought by a group of people, a sector, an organisation, etc*)

3. We are currently operating at _____ _____ , which means that we can afford to keep prices lower for our clients. (*the most efficient level of production or output, with the result that production costs are kept to a minimum*)

4. She works on an _____ _____ in a factory that makes electronic goods. (*a production system where a product moves slowly through a factory as new parts are added to it*)

5. We do not allow visitors to come onto the factory floor, but you can view our range of _____ _____ in the showroom. (*complete products that are ready to sell*)

6. The company had to put out a _____ _____ to its customers when several potentially dangerous faults were discovered. (*the removal from sale of an item that might be dangerous to the people who have bought it*)

7. We will be unable to compete successfully in the domestic market unless we reduce our costs by taking advantage of _____ _____. (*the manufacture of goods in another country for import to the domestic market*)

8. Our company builds _____ _____ into most of its electronic products, so that our customers are forced or obliged to update them more often. (*designing products so that they have a limited lifespan and so need to be replaced more often*)

9. We make packaging for frozen food, and are an important part of the _____ _____ for the industry. (*the manufacturers, wholesalers, distributors, etc, who make, deliver and sell products to customers*)

10. None of our products are allowed to leave the factory unless there are _____ _____ present. (*having no faults*)

11. Without effective _____ _____, we will not be able to produce enough goods to keep up with demand. (*assigning people and machines to projects in a way that optimises production and results*)

12. The manufacture of most items relies on a reliable source of _____ _____ such as wood, iron ore or crude petroleum. (*basic items which have to be treated in some way before they can be used*)

13. If _____ _____ can be kept to a minimum, we can keep market prices at a minimum. (*the money needed to make a product*)

For reference see *Dictionary of Business - 4th edition* (A&C Black Publishers Ltd, 978-0-713-67918-2)

14. We don't check every item before we send it for sale. We usually find that _____ _____ gives us a good idea of quality. (*testing a few items from one batch of products before they are sent for sale*)

15. Our company takes _____ _____ very seriously: we never start a project without working out how many people it will need, and the equipment they will require. (*measuring the amount of work that can be done within a certain amount of time, and how many people, machines, etc, it will need*)

Exercise 2: Look at the definitions in sentences 1 – 16, and decide what is being described in each case. The words you need are in the box (you will need to use some of these words more than once). There are 8 words that do not match any of the definitions.

Write your answers in the appropriate space in the table on the next page. In cases where more than one word is needed, do not put any gaps between those words in the table. If you complete it correctly, you will reveal a three-word expression in the shaded vertical column that refers to a production system where work is split up into clearly defined tasks and areas of responsibility.

and	backlog	bar	batch	centralised	continuous	coding	demand
	development	down	error	first	global	goods	in	improvement
intermediate	just	logistics	made	maintenance	margin	of	operating
order	out	outsourcing	packaging	parts	preventive	pricing	production
	research	sourcing	spare	stockout	supplier	supply	time	to

1. The process of attaching machine-readable lines on a product, product part or package, which can then be read by a computer. (*2 words*)

2. The task of managing the movement, storage and processing of materials and information in a supply chain. (*1 word*)

3. The servicing of factory machines and other equipment that is carried out before a fault develops. (*2 words*)

4. Goods that are bought for use in the production of other products. (*2 words*)

5. A situation where a particular component or part has been used up and has not been replenished (often as a result of poor inventory control). (*1 word*)

6. A period during which a machine is not available because it is being serviced or has broken down. (*2 words*)

7. An allowance made for the possibility of mistakes (for example, a miscalculation in a calculation) (*3 words*)

8. A production system in which goods are made or purchased just before they are needed. (*3 words*)

9. An item that is produced in response to the request of a particular client or customer. (*3 words*)

10. A method of stock control in which the stock of a product in store is used before more recently produced or purchased stock. (*4 words*)

11. The amount of goods available for sale and the level of consumer need for those goods. (*3 words*)

12. Finding out facts and information before making a new product, or improving a current one. (*3 words*)

13. A contract in which the supplier charges the customer the same price for delivery of goods anywhere in the world. (*2 words*)

For reference see *Dictionary of Business - 4th edition* (A&C Black Publishers Ltd, 978-0-713-67918-2)

14. The practice of obtaining services from other companies rather than using in-house services (including production services) (*1 word*)

15. Making production processes and products better over a period of time in order to increase quality and reduce waste. (*2 words*)

16. Pieces of machinery that are used to replace parts of a machine that are broken or faulty. (*2 words*)

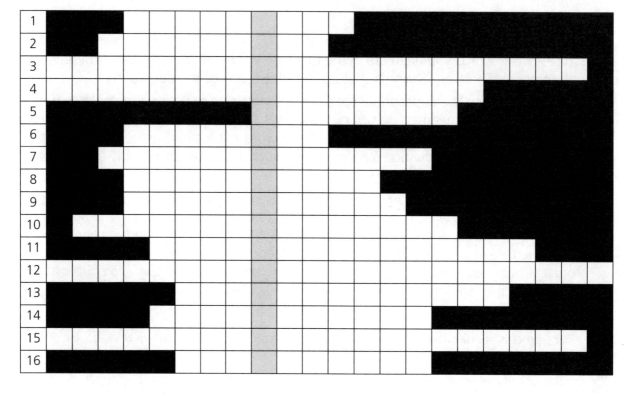

Exercise 3: Here are some more word pairs associated with production and operations. Match a word on the left with its 'partner' on the right. There are two words on the left that do not have a partner.

automatic	assembly
batch	book
buffer	capacity
bottleneck	control
buying	floor
centralised	forwarder
cluster	line
contract	manager
forward	manufacturing
freight	price
list	production
order	purchasing
paced	sampling
quality	scheduling
shop	stock
surplus	
warehousing	

For reference see *Dictionary of Business - 4th edition* (A&C Black Publishers Ltd, 978-0-713-67918-2)

Complete the conversation with words or expressions from the box.

advance	application	basic salary	benefits	candidate	colleagues
commencing	commission	covering letter	CV	drive (noun)	experience
incentive	increment	interview	leading (adjective)	motivate	post qualified
relocation allowance	responsibilities	rewards package	team	vacancy	

Sandra:	What are you reading?
Terry:	I'm looking at the jobs pages in the paper. There's something here I like the sound of. Modus International, a **1.**_____ supplier of car parts, has a **2.**_____ for the **3.**_____ of Sales Manager in their Brighton office.
Sandra:	That sounds like your kind of job. When does it begin?
Terry:	Let me see. Er, **4.**_____ April 1st, it says here. That's in three weeks' time.
Sandra:	You'd better get your **5.**_____ in, if you're interested. What else does it say about the job?
Terry:	It says that the successful **6.**_____ should be suitably **7.**_____ and should have had extensive **8.**_____ in sales management.
Sandra:	That sounds perfect. You've got a University degree in Business Management, and you've been working in sales for more than five years.
Terry:	I suppose so. It also says that he or she should be able to work as part of a **9.**_____, and should have **10.**_____ and the ability to **11.**_____ and inspire his or her **12.**_____.
Sandra:	Well, that's great! You've always got on with the people you work with, and everyone is always saying how you're able to encourage people to work harder.
Terry:	That's true. It also says that the **13.**_____ include liaising with colleagues around the country, training new staff and presenting a full report to the board of directors twice a year.
Sandra:	It all sounds quite good. What's the company offering in return?
Terry:	The **14.**_____ they're offering looks very attractive. It includes a **15.**_____ of £25000 per annum…
Sandra:	What does that mean?
Terry:	Well, that's the minimum amount of money that you can earn during the year. In addition to that, they're offering 10% **16.**_____ on all sales made.
Sandra:	Well, that's a good **17.**_____. The more you work, the more you sell. And the more you sell, the more money you'll make!
Terry:	Exactly. There's also a guaranteed annual **18.**_____ of £1500, and a **19.**_____ of £2500.
Sandra:	What's that for?
Terry:	To pay me for moving to the area, finding somewhere to live, and so on. Oh, and there are other **20.**_____, such as a company car, free medical and dental insurance and free meals in the canteen. It also says that there is room to **21.**_____, so I might end up with an even better job within the company.
Sandra:	So what should you do if you're interested in applying for the job?
Terry:	It says I should send my **22.**_____, together with a **23.**_____, to their head office in Sheffield. If the company is interested, they'll contact me to arrange an **24.**_____ at one of their offices nearer home.

For reference see *Dictionary of Business - 4th edition* (A&C Black Publishers Ltd, 978-0-713-67918-2)

Recruitment 2: The recruitment process

This text about the recruitment process below has been divided into three parts. Complete each part with the words and expressions in the boxes. The first answer for each part has been done for you. Some of the words and expressions have already appeared in *Recruitment 1* on the previous page.

Part 1

> affirmative recruitment   applicants   appointments   benefits   description
> disabilities   discrimination   equal opportunities   experience   externally
> institutional agency   increments   internally   job centres   journals   leave
> personal qualities   private recruitment agency   qualifications   recruit
> recruitment agency   rewards   situations vacant   staff   ~~vacancy~~

When a company or organisation has a **1.** _vacancy_ for a job, and it needs to **2.**_____a new member of **3.**_____, it usually advertises the post. It does this **4.**_____ (for example, in the company magazine or on a company notice board) or **5.**_____, either in the **6.**_____ or **7.**_____section of a newspaper, in specialist trade **8.**_____or through a **9.**_____ which helps people to find employment. There are two main types of agency. The first of these is the **10.**_____, usually found in a school or university. These work closely with employers to let potential employees know about the jobs that are on offer (also included in this category are **11.**_____, which are provided by the state, and which can be found in most main towns in Britain and other countries). The second is the **12.**_____, which are independent companies, and employers have to pay these agencies for each employee they successfully provide.

A job advertisement has to give an accurate **13.**_____ of the job and what it requires from the **14.**_____ (the people who are interested in the post). These requirements might include **15.**_____ (academic, vocational and professional), work **16.**_____ in similar lines of work, and certain **17.**_____ (for example, it might say that you need to be practical, professional and have a sense of humour). The advertisement will also specify what **18.**_____ (basic salary, commission, regular **19.**_____, etc) and **20.**_____ (paid **21.**_____, free medical insurance, company car, etc) the company can offer in return. The advertisement must be careful it does not break employment laws concerning sex and racial **22.**_____: some companies emphasise in their job advertisements that they are **23.**_____ employers (or **24.**_____ employers in the USA), which means that they will employ people regardless of their sex, skin colour, religion, **25.**_____, etc.

Part 2

> application   aptitude   board   candidates   covering   ~~CV~~
> group-situational   health screening   in-basket   introduction   medical
> one-to-one   pre-selection   psychometric   short-list   turn down

For reference see *Dictionary of Business - 4th edition* (A&C Black Publishers Ltd, 978-0-713-67918-2)

The job advertisement will usually ask people interested in the post to send their **1.** _____CV_____ with a **2.**_____ letter or a letter of **3.**_____, or they will ask people to write or call for an **4.**_____ form. The managers of the company will look at these, and go through a **5.**_____ procedure, where they choose or **6.**_____ applicants. They then prepare a **7.**_____ of possible **8.** : these are the people who will then be invited for an interview. Interviews usually take one of two forms. The first is the **9.**_____ interview, with one applicant and one employer talking together. The second is the **10.**_____ interview, with one applicant being interviewed by several people at once.

There may also be tests to see whether the applicant is suitable for the post. There are several of these, including **11.**_____ tests (which consider psychological aspects of the applicant), **12.** tests, (which test the applicant's skills and knowledge, and his / her potential for acquiring more skills and knowledge), **13.**_____ tests (where several applicants are put into an imaginary situation and decide how to deal with it), and **14.**_____ tests (in which an applicant has to deal with a number of imaginary tasks similar to those s/he would face in the job). Applicants may also have to go for a **15.**_____ test (also called a **16.**_____) to see whether they are healthy enough to do their job.

Part 3

appearance	circumstances	disposition	fixed-term	follow-up
induction programme		intelligence	interests	offered	open-ended
potential	probationary	references	~~seven-point plan~~	skills	temporary

Many employers use a **1.** _seven-point plan_ when they recruit for a new post. They look at different aspects of the applicant to decide whether or not s/he has the correct **2.**_____ for the job. These include physical **3.**_____ (for example, is the applicant smart and well-presented?), educational qualifications, general **4.**_____, special **5.**_____, hobbies and outside **6.**_____, mental and emotional **7.**_____ and family **8.**_____.

If a candidate gets through the above stages, s/he will be asked to provide **9.**_____from people who know him / her, and if these are positive, s/he is then **10.**_____ the post. Before s/he actually starts working, s/he may go through an **11.**_____ to learn more about the company and the post. Sometimes, s/he may be given a **12.**_____ contract and have to complete a **13.** period, where the employers make sure that s/he is suitable for the job before being offered an **14.** or **15.**_____ contract. After s/he has been with the company for a while, there might be a **16.**___ session, to assess how s/he is getting on in the post.

41

For reference see *Dictionary of Business - 4th edition* (A&C Black Publishers Ltd, 978-0-713-67918-2)

Exercise 1: In this contract of employment, there are a lot of vocabulary mistakes. Either a word is spelt incorrectly, the form of the word is wrong, or a wrong word has been used. Identify and correct these words. Some of the mistakes occur more than once in the contract.

1.		Term and conditionals of employment
2.	Name of employ:	Dilligaf Toys plc
3.	Name of employed:	Sarah Ramus
4.	Job titel:	Regional Production Manager.
5.	Job descriptive:	To oversee the work of the Production Department.
6.	Job locally:	Head Office, London. Branches in South and South-East.
7.	Celery:	£35,000 per anum (payable monthly in rears)
8.	Started date:	1 August 2007.
9.	Hours of labour:	Full time. 9.00 – 5.00 Monday until Friday.
10.	Undertime:	Extra hours worked will be paid at the normal hourly rat. Saturdays will be paid at time x 1 ½, Sundays at time x2.
11.	Holiday enticement:	21 days per anum, plus bank holidays.
12.	Absent from work:	If for any reason you cannot come to work, you should telephone the central manager as soon as possible.
13.	Pension sceme:	The company operates its own pension sceme which is open to all employs.
14.	Dissiplinary and grieving procedures:	Information on these procedures are provided in the staff handybook, together with information on all company police.
15.	Probbation:	All appointments are subjective to three months' probbation, during which time employees may be terminated with two weeks' note on either side.
16.	Terminator:	After successful completion of the probbation period, the note period will be three months.
17.	Referrals:	All apointments are subject to satisfactory referrals.
18.	Singed _____ *Sarah Ramus* _____	Date: *21 June 2007*

Exercise 2: Read this informal discussion, in which the person who signed the contract in Exercise 1 is telling their friend about their new job. Complete the gaps with an appropriate word or expression from the box. Some of these words appeared in Exercise 1.

For reference see *Dictionary of Business - 4th edition* (A&C Black Publishers Ltd, 978-0-713-67918-2)

accountability	agree	based	branches	commission	consult	deal with
delegate	departments	ensure	evaluate	full-time	head office	hours	inspect
key responsibilities	leave *(noun)*	negotiate	nine to five	per annum	produce
recommend	report to	responsible	salary	supervise	title	visit

James: Hi, Sarah. How's the new job going?

Sarah: Oh, not too bad. I'm still trying to find my feet, though.

James: Tell me a bit about it.

Sarah: Well, my official job _____ is Regional Production Manager, which means that my main _____ is to _____ the work of the production department.

James: Where are you _____?

Sarah: Most of my work is done at the _____ in central London, but I also have to spend time at our various _____ and _____ in the area. There are several of these in the South and South-East.

James: Who do you _____?

Sarah: The Central Production Manager. Tom Atkinson, his name is. I've only met him a couple of times, but he seems nice enough. We meet once a month to _____ each other on major issues. We _____ the current state of production, and I _____ any changes that I think need to be made

James: And what about the _____?

Sarah: Pretty typical for this kind of job. I'm on a _____ contract, which means I work from Monday to Friday, _____. And occasionally I have to go in at the weekend, too. I get 21 days_____ a year, plus bank holidays.

James: Not bad. And your _____? If you don't mind me asking?

Sarah: No, not at all. I get £35,000 _____, plus expenses, _____ for reaching targets, overtime pay and so on.

James: That's pretty good for a job that just involves checking things are running smoothly.

Sarah: Well, there's more to my job than just that. I do have several other _____.

James: Such as?

Sarah: First of all I have to _____ product specifications with sales departments and time schedules with the stock control department. Then I need to _____ that the product is manufactured according to agreed specifications, and I also have to _____ the quality of the finished product.

James: That's all?

Sarah: No. I also need to _____ with our suppliers on prices for our base materials, _____ those suppliers on a regular basis to check the quality of the base materials...

James: Do you have a car for that?

Sarah: Oh yes, the company provides me with one. I also have to _____ problems as they arise on a day-to-day basis, and _____ regular sales reports for the Directors.

James: Anything else?

Sarah: Well, on top of everything else, I'm _____ for managing 10 machinists, 3 trainees, 2 cleaners and 2 security guards.

James: That sounds like a lot of work for one person. Can you _____ any of it?

Sarah: Unfortunately no. I have to do it all myself!

43

For reference see *Dictionary of Business - 4th edition* (A&C Black Publishers Ltd, 978-0-713-67918-2)

Sales and marketing 1

In the following sentences, the enthusiastic marketing manager of a mobile phone company is telling her team about the company's latest model of mobile phone. However, each sentence contains a spelling mistake. Identify and correct the word in each case.

1. Everybody says that the market for mobile phones is very cowded, and there is no more room or demand for new products.

2. However, we believe we've found a nich in the market for something a little bit different: a mobile phone with an infra-red camera that lets you see in the dark. Impressive, eh?

3. However, this isn't its only uniqe selling point.

4. It also has a huge range of other feachures, including a built-in navigation system, a scanner, a photo-editing suite, a dictionary and translator and even a thermometer.

5. We call it the 'Ultimafone®', and we've just applied for a patient so that no-one else can copy it.

6. It was conceived by our inovative designs team, led by the brilliant Kevin Anorak.

7. We plan to lunch it early in the New Year.

8. You'll find the 'Ultimafone®' on page 1 of our latest mobile phones brocure.

9. - As you can see, it's the ultimate must-have opmarket accessory.

10. We made the decision to start making it after extensive reserch into what people wanted from a mobile phone in the 21st century.

11. Of course, we won't sell many without a great deal of advertiseing.

12. As a result, we're starting a major campain to let the public know all about it.

13. We're going to premote the 'Ultimafone®' any way we can.

14. There are going to be comercials on all of the main radio stations and television channels.

15. In fact, we're hoping to get at least five spouts on each of the major channels during prime-time viewing.

16. All the daily newspapers and major magazines will carry full-page advertments.

17. There will be plenty of product pacement in some of the biggest films of the year.

18. You won't be able to walk down the street without seeing one of our giant billyboards.

19. And you won't even be able to visit the Internet without our plop-ups coming up on your screen all the time!

20. We're also going to send mailshoots to everyone who has ever bought one of our phones in the past.

21. And naturally we'll be making some sponsership deals with some of the country's major sporting teams.

22. If we're lucky, we might even get a famous rock star, actor or sports personality to endoarse it for us.

23. After all, you can't beat an opinon leader for really helping to make a new product take off successfully.

For reference see *Dictionary of Business - 4th edition* (A&C Black Publishers Ltd, 978-0-713-67918-2)

24. There will also be big posters at every pont of sale (including department stores and music stores).

25. In fact, there probably won't be a single major retale outlet anywhere in the country that doesn't sell the 'Ultimafone®'!

26. Our expert sales team - that's you - will be there to give potential customers your pich and persuade them that the 'Ultimafone®' is just what they need.

27. There will be lots of special offers, including miscounts on phone and talk-time packages.

28. There will also be lots of giveways: free hands-free kits, free phone covers, free ringtones, and so on.

29. Sales won't just be limited to the dommestic market.

30. We believe that the 'Ultimafone®' will really catch on in the expot market as well.

31. In fact, our overseas raps are already packing their suitcases and booking their flight tickets.

32. Eventually we hope to have the 'Ultimafone®' made under franshise in mainland Europe, the Far East and South America.

33. We're so confident of the reliability of the 'Ultimafone®' that they will all carry a free 3-year guarantea.

34. That's not bad, considering the where and tear that can be expected from the customers on an item such as this.

35. You might also like to know that in addition to the phone itself, there will be a whole range of 'Ultimafone®' merchantizing, including 'Ultimafone®' T-shirts, 'Ultimafone®' trainers and even 'Ultimafone®' biscuits!

36. They will all carry the soon-to-be famous 'Ultimafone®' brant name.

37. They will all display a distinctive 'Ultimafone®' loco.

38. And they will all come in an attractive, instantly-recognisable 'Ultimafone®' pakaging.

39. Our latest cattalog has the whole range!

40. We think it's the best invention since the microchip, although obviously some people will tell you that it's just hyp, and we're making a lot of fuss about nothing.

41. They'll say that the 'Ultimafone®' is nothing more than a fat, and that this time next year nobody will want one!

42. However, I just know it will sell well, and I bet our competiton is getting really worried!

43. In the war for new customers, we're going to tramp them!

44. However, we mustn't be too complacent. We will be trucking our buying public over the next year or so to see how they react to the 'Ultimafone®'.

45. So get out there, and canvince as many people as possible that the 'Ultimafone®' is the only mobile phone they'll ever need!

Also see *Sales and marketing 2* on the next page.

For reference see *Dictionary of Business - 4th edition* (A&C Black Publishers Ltd, 978-0-713-67918-2)

Rearrange the letters in **bold** in these definitions and explanations to make words connected with sales and marketing. Then write these words in the appropriate space in the grid. If you do this correctly, you will reveal a three-word idiomatic expression in the shaded vertical strip that marketing people use to describe people who are easy marketing targets because they are already thinking of buying a product or service.

1. The process of a product going out of date because of progress in design or technology, and therefore becoming less useful or valuable, is known as **bencsoslecoe**.
2. **moonPtior** is the means of conveying the message about a product or service to potential customers (for example, publicity, a sales campaign, television commercials, etc).
3. **ehlaWoles** is a word referring to the business of buying goods from manufacturers and selling them in large quantities to retailers, who then sell in smaller quantities to the public.
4. **magencrkhiBn** is the system of measuring the performance of a company against the performance of other companies in the same sector.
5. Unsolicited mail advertising, and especially email advertising, is known as **amsp** (named after a famous American brand of tinned meat).
6. The transfer of rights to manufacture or market a particular product to another individual or organisation through a legal arrangement or contract is called **niligesnc**.
7. The brand name of a product that is recognised around the world is known as a **boglla** brand.
8. A **ephlrsadei** is a retail outlet distributing, selling and servicing products (especially cars) on behalf of a manufacturer.
9. A **wdorknma** is the reduction of the price of something to less than its usual price.
10. When a new product or service is tested on a small group of consumers in order to try to find out the reactions of a larger group of consumers, this is known as **pigslman**.
11. The adding of new types of products to the range already made is known as **avidfictionsier**.
12. **mingerkeaTlet** is the selling of a product or service by telephone.
13. An organisation that delivers products to retailers on behalf of a manufacturer is called a **isorditbtru**.
14. A **eberife** is an informal word for a product or service that is given away, usually to encourage people to buy a bigger product or service, or to advertise that product or service (for example, a pen with the company name on).
15. In radio, television and cinema advertising, **tamirei** is the amount of time given to an advertisement.

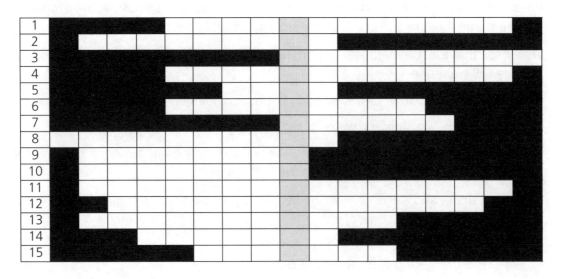

Also see *Sales and marketing 3* on the next page.

For reference see *Dictionary of Business - 4th edition* (A&C Black Publishers Ltd, 978-0-713-67918-2)

Match each definition in sentences 1 – 32 with an appropriate word 'pair' connected with sales and marketing. The first word of each pair can be found hidden in the top box, and the second word can be found hidden in the bottom box. These words can be found by reading from left to right (⇨), and / or from top to bottom (⇩). The first one has been done as an example.

(Note that in some cases the same word may be needed more than once, but will only appear once in each grid).

C	Q	P	W	E	P	R	O	W	N	T	Y	U
R	I	R	O	P	U	M	A	P	R	I	C	E
I	S	E	D	C	B	A	F	R	G	A	L	H
S	J	M	K	O	L	I	C	O	L	D	I	L
I	Z	I	S	R	I	L	U	D	X	D	E	C
S	V	U	A	P	C	I	S	U	B	E	N	N
M	Q	M	L	O	W	N	T	C	E	D	T	N
R	T	P	E	R	T	G	O	T	R	A	D	E
Y	A	R	S	A	U	B	M	A	R	K	E	T
I	R	E	O	T	P	R	E	W	A	R	D	W
A	G	S	S	E	D	A	R	L	O	S	S	O
F	E	S	G	H	J	N	W	H	I	T	E	R
K	T	R	A	D	E	D	L	H	I	G	H	K
F	O	C	U	S	C	O	N	S	U	M	E	R
Z	X	B	R	E	A	K	C	V	B	N	M	Q

D	G	D	Q	W	G	O	O	D	S	L	E	A	P
R	R	E	P	R	E	S	S	U	R	E	R	W	L
I	O	L	A	H	O	U	S	E	T	A	L	A	D
V	U	E	B	R	A	N	D	Y	U	D	O	R	I
E	P	G	A	I	O	P	C	A	R	E	Y	E	F
N	F	A	N	S	C	H	E	M	E	R	A	N	F
A	O	T	D	V	A	L	U	E	S	W	L	E	E
M	R	I	O	D	L	F	A	I	R	A	T	S	R
A	E	O	N	F	L	E	A	D	E	R	Y	S	E
R	C	N	M	B	A	S	E	I	M	A	G	E	N
K	A	L	E	A	D	E	R	S	H	I	P	G	T
E	S	E	N	S	E	N	S	I	T	I	V	E	I
T	T	V	T	M	A	R	K	E	T	I	N	G	A
H	J	E	K	R	E	L	A	T	I	O	N	G	T
L	Z	N	P	R	O	T	E	C	T	I	O	N	I
X	M	A	N	A	G	E	M	E	N	T	C	V	O
R	E	L	E	A	S	E	T	O	F	F	E	R	N

1. An increase in the attractiveness to customers of a product or service which is achieved by adding something to it (for example, a computer might come with pre-loaded software, a printer, scanner, etc). = ***added value***

2. A large exhibition and meeting for advertising and selling a specific type of product.

3. A long-term customer preference for a particular product or service (for example, someone who always buys Mazda cars because he thinks they are better than other cars on the market).

4. A carefully selected representative range of consumers used for the purposes of providing feedback on likes and preferences.

5. To reach the point at which revenue (the amount of money received for selling something) is equal to the costs of production.

For reference see *Dictionary of Business - 4th edition* (A&C Black Publishers Ltd, 978-0-713-67918-2)

6.   A system that gives incentives to customers to continue using the same shop or service (for example, by collecting points that they can redeem on future purchases).

7.   A competition between companies to get a larger market share by cutting prices.

8.   Machines which are used in the kitchen, such as washing machines, refrigerators, etc.

9.   An organisation that specialises in planning, creating and implementing direct mail campaigns for clients.

10.   A marketing technique that promotes and emphasises a product's difference from other products of a similar nature.

11.   The activity of looking after customers so that they do not become dissatisfied.

12.   A telephone call or sales visit where the sales person has no appointment and the client is not an established customer.

13.   Actions taken by an organisation to protect itself when unexpected events or situations occur that could threaten its success or continued operation (for example, a competitor selling a better product at a lower price).

14.   The regular customers of an organisation or professional person.

15.   The selling of goods or services through a linked group of self-employed agents or representatives.

16.   An item in a shop that is sold below cost price in order to attract customers into the shop.

17.   A prediction of future sales based mainly on past sales performance.

18.   A two-word adjective used to describe a sales technique in which a customer is forced to buy something that he / she does not really want.

19.   The level of recognition that consumers have of a company name (or its products) and its specific category (for example, most people know that McDonalds® sell fast food, especially burgers).

20.   The practice of building up and keeping contacts with customers, clients, the general public, etc.

21.   A product or service which sells the most in a market.

22.   A sheet giving news about something (for example, a new product) which is sent to newspapers and television and radio stations so that they can use the information.

23.   A two-word adjective used to describe a product or service for which sales remain constant no matter what its price because it is essential to buyers.

24.   The ending of the manufacture and sale of a product.

25.   The safeguarding of customers' interests in terms of quality, price and safety.

26.   A group of manufacturers or suppliers who visit another country to increase export business.

27.   An idea which a company would like the public to have of it.

28.   The establishment of price levels in a market by a dominant company or brand.

29.   The people to whom a company is planning to sell its goods or services.

30.   A sales promotion technique in which customers are offered a 'free gift'.

31.   The name of a store which is used on products which are specially packed (and sometimes produced) for that store.

32.   Using your knowledge of your customers in order to determine the corporate strategy of your company or organisation.

For reference see *Dictionary of Business* - 4th edition (A&C Black Publishers Ltd, 978-0-713-67918-2)

Exercise 1: Look at sentences 1 – 22. These can either be completed with a word from box A *or* a word with a similar meaning from box B. Identify both the words that could be used. In some cases, you will need to add an -*s* to one or both of the words when you put them into the sentence.

A	B
acclaim administration agenda appointment benefit charisma choice code cooperation customer discipline discount drop fault liability opposition proof proximity requirement staff takeover work	acquisition advantage (personal) appeal client closeness collaboration decline defect employment evidence meeting option order patron personnel praise prerequisite receivership reduction resistance responsibility rule schedule

1.   We have a very busy _____ / _____ today, so I suggest we start as soon as possible.

2.   After two financially disastrous years, the company went into _____ / _____ .

3.   We need to maintain _____ / _____ on the factory floor at all times, otherwise there are increased risks of an accident occurring.

4.   Several employees were made redundant following EZPrint's _____ / _____ of Colourcom.

5.   There has been a sharp _____ / _____ in the number of people attending the staff development sessions.

6.   The latest computer program has several _____ / _____ which need to be sorted out before it can be put onto the market.

7.   There has been a lot of _____ / _____ to the new compulsory overtime plan.

8.   Despite government reassurances, there is no _____ / _____ that standards of living have improved.

9.   Repeated orders are eligible for a 10% _____ / _____ on wholesale prices.

10.   The hotel is popular with business people because of its _____ / _____ to the central business district.

11.   I can't see you this afternoon because I have a / an _____ / _____ with the Board of Directors.

12.   A lot of our regular _____ / _____ say that they are unhappy with the speed of our service.

13.   When the company begins operations, it hopes to provide _____ / _____ for 300 people.

14.   There are several _____ / _____ to working from home: you save on travel costs, for one thing.

15.   If you want the job, a working knowledge of German is one of the main _____ / _____.

16.   Our latest range of language-learning products has received widespread _____ / _____ in the press, and is expected to help us become a market leader.

17.   The company _____ / _____ state(s) that no employee can leave his or her work station without asking for permission.

18.   The management accepts no _____ / _____ for any damage to vehicles in the car park.

19.   There are two _____ / _____ available to us: close the company or move to another locality.

20.   All _____ / _____ are requested to attend tomorrow's meeting, which will begin at 2pm.

21.   Thanks to our _____ / _____ with several affiliated companies, we have increased our turnover by 37%.

22.   We believe that the new manager's lack of _____ / _____ will have a negative effect on sales.

For reference see *Dictionary of Business - 4th edition* (A&C Black Publishers Ltd, 978-0-713-67918-2)

Exercise 2: Instructions as above.

A	B
achievement advertising assignment calibre category customer disparity ending entitlement notion outlet priority problem proceeds proficiency question review revision specialist strategy term ultimatum	accomplishment change classification complication condition difference earnings expert final demand idea intellect and ability job patron plan precedence publicity query right shop skill termination write-up

1.   Our latest range of products has received several favourable _____ / _____ in the press, and should be a firm favourite with the 18 – 24 age group.

2.   Our latest model is excellent, but without adequate _____ / _____, we won't make enough to cover production costs.

3.   _____ / _____ are requested not to smoke in the restaurant.

4.   The hotel has several room _____ / _____, including five family rooms and two honeymoon suites.

5.   Poor long-term sales figures resulted in the _____ / _____ of the contract and the closure of two offices.

6.   If you leave the company, you will lose your _____ / _____ to a share of the profits.

7.   We would very much appreciate having somebody of your _____ / _____ working for us: you would be of great benefit to the company.

8.   We called in a health and safety _____ / _____ to examine the building for any potential problems.

9.   He was given the _____ / _____ of dealing with the press and keeping the public informed about new developments.

10.   The new manager has a strange _____ / _____ that all employees are potentially dishonest.

11.   She hasn't reached the required level of _____ / _____ in typing, and will have to repeat that section of the training course.

12.   His promotion to director was a remarkable _____ / _____ for someone so young.

13.   The bank gave us a / an _____ / _____: pay back the money or face immediate closure.

14.   Despite several changes to the pay structure, there is still a _____ / _____ in pay between graduate trainees and non-graduates.

15.   All _____ / _____ from the sale of the building will be re-invested in the company.

16.   We advise you to read the _____ / _____ of the contract carefully, and contact us if you disagree with any of the points covered.

17.   If you have any _____ / _____, please ask a member of staff.

18.   Selfwood's operates several _____ / _____ where you can buy a selection of our own goods along with a large range of branded varieties.

19.   We had hoped that everything would run smoothly, but unfortunately there have been several _____ / _____.

20.   Our _____ / _____ is to wait for prices to fall before putting the product onto the market.

21.   Advertising is currently our main concern, and it should take _____ / _____ over everything else.

22.   Is it necessary to make any _____ / _____ to the plan, or should we keep it as it is?

For reference see *Dictionary of Business - 4th edition* (A&C Black Publishers Ltd, 978-0-713-67918-2)

Look at the words and expressions in *italics*, and then rearrange the letters in **bold** that follow each expression to make a word with the same or a similar meaning *in the same context*. Use these words to complete the crossword on the next page.

Across (⇨)

(4)	*Help* a customer.	**ssaits**
(9)	*Agree* to do something.	**nnscoet**
(11)	*Make* something clearer.	**aylrifc**
(12)	*Book* a restaurant table.	**veerres**
(13)	*Control* a process or activity.	**ergateul**
(14)	*Examine* information in detail.	**alseyan**
(16)	*Collect* information.	**tgaehr**
(17)	*Speak* to an audience.	**rsedsad**
(24)	*Choose* something.	**celste**
(26)	*Produce* or *make* good sales of a product.	**ereengat**
(28)	*Manage* or *organise* a department.	**stainierdm**
(30)	*Verify* something is true.	**nmfcori**
(33)	*Examine* financial accounts.	**duita**
(34)	*Give* information or instructions to your staff.	**erbfi**
(35)	*Tell* somebody about an event that has happened.	**taeler**
(37)	*Measure* the effect of something.	**nafytqui**
(39)	*Remove* something from a sum of money.	**cdutde**
(41)	*Require* somebody to do something.	**lbioeg**
(42)	*Increase* your area of operations.	**iwned**
(43)	*Take on* new staff.	**mleyop**

Down (⇩)

(1)	*Finish making* plans for something.	**ilifsena**
(2)	*Suggest* something *without saying it directly*.	**yplim**
(3)	*Ask* somebody *for advice*.	**ucsotnl**
(4)	*Make* a process *go faster*.	**aeclrcteae**
(5)	*Deal with* a problem.	**leahdn**
(6)	*Keep* something for future use.	**etrina**
(7)	*Come to* an interview.	**teadnt**
(8)	*Give* or *take* a message to somebody.	**ecvyon**
(9)	*Make up for* something you have done wrong.	**pensacteom**
(10)	*Reveal* information to somebody.	**esolcsid**
(12)	*Settle* an argument or disagreement.	**veslroe**
(15)	*Replace* something with something similar.	**tetubstsui**
(18)	*Firmly tell* somebody your terms and conditions.	**tadteic**
(19)	*Firmly state* your opinion.	**sraset**
(20)	*Promote* a product.	**tiarseedv**
(21)	*Prevent* a strike from taking place.	**rvate**
(22)	*Use up* all your resources.	**etdeepl**
(23)	*Recover* lost money or property.	**airclem**
(25)	*Approve of* a decision.	**oresend**
(27)	*To not allow* smoking in a public place.	**hpobitir**
(29)	*Have an effect on* someone or something.	**ncfiunlee**
(31)	*Give* a contract to a company.	**radwa**
(32)	*Try* to do a difficult job.	**ptetmat**
(36)	*Check* facts *to see if they are true*.	**scenraiat**
(38)	*Obtain* or *get* information	**uciraqe**
(40)	*Account for* something that has happened.	**pixlnae**

For reference see *Dictionary of Business - 4th edition* (A&C Black Publishers Ltd, 978-0-713-67918-2)

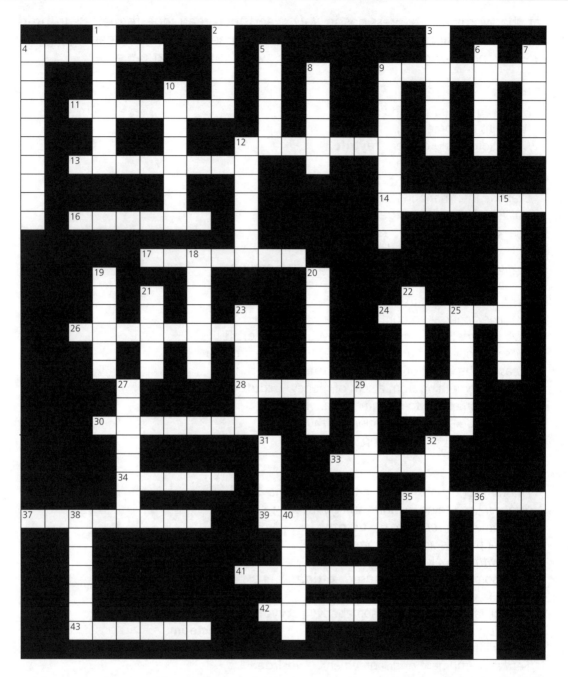

Note that using a word with a similar meaning to another word does not always mean using that word in exactly the same way. For example: you can '*prevent a strike from taking place*' or you can '*avert a strike*' (not '*avert a strike from taking place*'); you can '*suggest something without saying it directly*' or you can '*imply something*' (not '*imply something without saying it directly*'). In these examples, the words at the end are not necessary because their meaning is carried in the main verb. This is one reason why you should always record words in context, and with an example that shows how they are used, so that when you use them yourself, you use them correctly.

Also note that some of these verbs can be used in more than one way. For example, you can *convey a message to someone*, or you can *convey goods from one place to another*.

For reference see *Dictionary of Business - 4th edition* (A&C Black Publishers Ltd, 978-0-713-67918-2)

Exercise 1: Match the words and expressions in **bold** in sentences 1 – 20 with words with the same or a similar meaning. These words can be found in the box by reading from left to right, and from right to left, in the direction of the arrows. However, the words in the box are <u>not</u> in the same order as the sentences they match.

START ⇨	a	b	r	u	p	t	r	e	s	o	l	u	t	e	b	a	s	i	c ⇒
⇐ r	c	s	u	o	l	u	p	r	c	s	e	v	i	s	n	e	t	x	e ⇒
⇘ u	c	i	a	l	m	a	n	d	a	t	o	r	y	o	u	t	d	a	t	e ⇒
⇐ i	t	r	e	p	t	n	a	d	n	u	b	a	t	n	a	r	b	i	v	d ⇐
⇘ n	e	n	t	d	i	s	c	o	u	r	t	e	o	u	s	o	v	e	r	a ⇒
⇐ t	s	i	s	n	o	c	n	i	d	e	t	c	i	r	t	s	e	r	l	l ⇐
⇘ e	n	t	a	d	e	q	u	a	t	e	t	h	o	r	o	u	g	h	i	n ⇒
FINISH	w	o	r	r	a	n	y	k	s	i	r	e	l	b	i	x	e	l	f ⇐

1.   We've carried out a **comprehensive** audit of our accounts, but haven't found any irregularities.

2.   Regular government health and safety inspections are **compulsory**.

3.   Despite several USP's* in our latest range, we can expect to face some **determined** competition from our rivals.

4.   We are unable to make a decision at this time as we do not have **enough** information.

5.   Your performance has become rather **erratic** recently, so we were wondering if you might benefit from going on a new training course.

6.   I'm not sure why your order was delayed for so long, but I assure you I will carry out a **full and detailed** investigation.

7.   We don't need to know all the details: try to give us a **general** idea.

8.   She's a very successful saleswoman, but I don't think she's particularly **honest and fair** with her clients.

9.   We have received a number of complaints about **impolite** sales people in our call centre.

10.   Employee access to the office after 6pm is strictly **limited and controlled**.

11.   People enjoy working in our department: the atmosphere in the office is really **lively**.

12.   Our department manager does a good job, although he is often criticised for his **old-fashioned** business ideas.

13.   There are **plenty of** opportunities for promotion within the company, provided you work hard enough.

14.   At the end of her presentation, there were several **relevant** questions from the audience.

15.   This schedule is too **rigid.** We need a bit of wiggle room** here.

16.   The company is unwilling to invest in financially **dangerous** projects.

17.   Free accommodation is provided for our employees. It is **simple but adequate**.

18.   Our profit margin has been very **small** over the last six months.

19.   We were ready to sign the contract when there was a **sudden** change of plan.

20.   There has been a lot of talk of redundancies, so this afternoon's meeting is **very important** for all those concerned.

* USP's: *unique selling points*.

** wiggle room: an informal expression for *time and flexibility*.

For reference see *Dictionary of Business - 4th edition* (A&C Black Publishers Ltd, 978-0-713-67918-2)

Exercise 2: Rearrange the letters in **bold** to make words that have the same or a similar meaning to the words and expressions in *italics*. Write each word in the table on the right of the page. The shaded letter in each word is the <u>first</u> letter of the next word. The first one has been done as an example.

1. A *likely* or *possible* job applicant. **ecivrosppte**

2. A product's *lasting* appeal. **ridugenn**

3. *Basic* computer skills. **utadirymren**

4. A *flourishing* IT business. **ringvith**

5. An *optional* dress code. **taurynlvo**

6. A *boring and repetitive* job. **outesdi**

7. A *constant and continuous* price rise. **saydte**

8. A flow of *unrelated* ideas. **spitdaear**

9. A *lucrative* venture. **opritleafb**

10. A *long* meeting. **glehnty**

11. A *small* charge for postage and packing. **monalin**

12. A *very important* part of something. **gainrtel**

13. An *outstanding* presentation. **nactexiolep**

14. Two *well-suited* organisations. **ticmpbleao**

15. An *observant* secretary. **cepetviper**

16. A *prompt* start to a meeting. **caputnlu**

17. A *valid* reason for doing something. **itemalegit**

18. A *hardworking* staff member. **iriustnusod**

19. *Punitive* action. **panscdiiylir**

20. A *creative* idea. **tivvenein**

21. A *significant* event. **naprotimt**

22. A *contemporary* approach to management. **omnedr**

23. A *varied* programme of events. **viseder**

24. A *well-run and productive* department. **fitefince**

25. *Easily changeable* working hours. **blleifex**

26. An *insolvent* company. **narubptk**

P	R	O	S	P	E	C	T	I	V	E
	E									

This letter is the first letter of number 1 ☞

For reference see *Dictionary of Business - 4th edition* (A&C Black Publishers Ltd, 978-0-713-67918-2)

Exercise 1: Complete these dialogues with words and expressions from the box.

automated services	call back	camping on the line	connect	convenient

automated services   call back   camping on the line   connect   convenient
cut off   dead   direct line   engaged   extension   get back   hang on   hash
hold the line   hung up   junk calls   message   on behalf of   on hold
put through   speaking   star   switchboard   tone   voicemail   zeroing out

1.   Caller: Could I speak to Jennifer Thompson in Accounts, please?

  Receptionist: I'm afraid her line is _____ at the moment. Shall I get her to _____ you _____ (you need one expression for these two gaps)?

2.   Caller: Oh, hello, could you _____ me _____ (you need one expression for these two gaps) to Ron Atkinson, please?

  Receptionist: Certainly. _____ please.

3.   Caller: Hello. Adam Harrison, please.

  Receptionist: He's out of the office, I'm afraid, but I can _____ you and you can leave a _____ on his _____, if you like.

  Caller: No, that's OK. I'll try again later. When would be a _____ time?

4.   Speaker 1:   Oh no, not again!

  Speaker 2:   What's up?

  Speaker 1:   I'm trying to call my credit card company, and I've got one of those stupid _____.

  Speaker 2:   Well, try _____. You might get through to a real human being.

  Speaker 1:   OK. Oh, the line's gone _____. I've been _____.

5.   Answering machine: Hello. This is Anthony Roberts. I'm not in the office at the moment, but if you leave your name and number after the _____, I'll _____ to you

6.   Speaker 1:   Bob's been on the phone for ages.

  Speaker 2:   I know. He's calling our supplier, but they've put him _____. He's been _____ for over ten minutes!

7.   Speaker 1:   *(Answering the phone)* Hello?

  Recorded message: Hello there. I'm Sandy from Moneygrubbers International, and I'm delighted to tell you that you have been personally selected from a list of literally millions to receive a fantastic travel offer…

  Speaker 2:   Who is it?

  Speaker 1:   *(putting down the phone)*: Oh, just one of those irritating _____.

8.   Mr Floyd: *(Answering the phone)* Hello?

  Telemarketer: Oh, hello. Could I speak to Mr Floyd, please?

  Mr Floyd: _____.

  Telemarketer: Good evening, Mr Floyd. I'm Tim Spanner, and I'm calling _____ Superglaze Windows. I was wondering if…

  Mr Floyd: (Says nothing, but puts the phone down)

  Telemarketer: Oh dear. That's the fifth one who's _____ on me today.

For reference see *Dictionary of Business - 4th edition* (A&C Black Publishers Ltd, 978-0-713-67918-2)

9.   Caller: Hello. Could I have Sarah Knowles' _____ please?

          Receptionist: Well, actually, she has a _____, which means you can by-pass the _____ the next time you call. If you _____ a moment, I'll get you her number.

10.   Speaker 1:   How do I access my messages on this phone?

         Speaker 2:   Press zero, then the _____ key. That's the little asterisk at the bottom of the keypad. Then press zero again, followed by the _____ key.

         Speaker 1:   Which one's that?

         Speaker 2:   The key with the four vertical and horizontal lines crossing one another.

Exercise 2. The popularity of SMS mobile phone text messaging has led to an increase in the use of certain abbreviations to communicate ideas (for example, 'FYI' means 'For your information'). Many of these are used by business people, not only in SMS messages, but also in emails and handwritten notes and messages.

Look at these messages, and try to decide what the abbreviations in **bold** mean. Choose the words you need from the box. You will need to use some words more than once.

a	am	as	back	be	business	by	crying	eyes	fact	for	glaze	
ha	hand	helps	hope	I	in	it	it's	keep	kidding	lawyer	loud	
matter	mind	my	not	of	on	only	opinion	other	out	over		
own	possible	respect	right	simple	soon	stupid	the	this	to			
	way	what	with	words	worth	your						

1.   We didn't make a profit last month. **AAMOF**, we lost almost £8000.

2.   I need a reply from you urgently. Please call me **ASAP**.

3.   Must go to a meeting now. **BRB**.

4.   Thanks for sending the contract. **BTW**, have you received our latest catalogue?

5.   I <u>still</u> haven't received your reply. **FCOL**, what are you playing at?

6.   I'm sorry the boss was so rude to you. **FWIW**, *I* think you've done a fantastic job.

7.   Thanks for lending me your mobile, but I'm afraid I've dropped it down the loo. **HHOK**! I'll bring it right back.

8.   Here's the information you asked for (see attachment). **HTH**.

9.   How should I know if our latest advertising campaign has broken the law. **IANAL**!

10.   You asked me what we should do about the fall in sales. **IMO**, we should meet and discuss this problem face to face.

11.   The papers we needed have finally arrived. **IOW**, we can get on with putting the project together at last.

12.   One bit of advice for the report you're writing: **KISS**!

13.   Have you seen his report? It's almost 200 pages long. Oh my god, **MEGO**!

14.   This is my project, not yours! Hands off, and **MYOB**!

15.   You *could* be wrong. **OTOH**, you're probably right.

16.   **WRT** your request for a day off next week, I'm afraid my answer is no.

For reference see *Dictionary of Business* - 4th edition (A&C Black Publishers Ltd, 978-0-713-67918-2)

Complete the sentences and definitions below with appropriate words, and use these words to complete the crossword grid on the next page. In each case, the first letter of each word you need is in the sentence / definition. The number and arrow after each gap show you where to put the word in the grid: ⇨= *across*, ⇩= *down*.

• When you bring goods into a country you i_____ (5⇨) them. When you send them out of a country you e_____ (15⇩) them.

• A group of manufacturers or suppliers who visit another country to increase their sales there is known as a trade d_____ (32⇨).

• C_____ (20⇨) – also called f_____ (26⇨) – is a general word for goods which are transported in a ship, plane etc. It is usually carried in a c_____ (14⇨) (= a very large metal case of a standard size).

• A bill of l_____ (3⇨) is a list of goods being transported, which the transporter gives to the person sending the goods, to show them that the goods have been loaded. The person receiving the goods should receive a p_____ (16⇩) list, showing them the goods that they should be receiving.

• A letter of c_____ (21⇩) – often abbreviated to *L/C* – is a document issued by a bank on behalf of a customer authorising payment to a supplier when conditions specified in the document are met.

• A p_____-_____ (24⇩) invoice is an invoice sent to a buyer before the goods are sent, so that payment can be made (or so that goods can be sent to a consignee who is not the buyer). (*note: write this as one word in your crossword grid: do not leave any spaces*)

• *COD* is a payment which is made for goods when they arrive. *COD* stands for *cash on d_____* (23⇨).

• A group of goods sent for sale by road, sea or air is called a c_____ (9⇩).

• *CIF* refers to the price a buyer has to pay for goods which have to be transported. It stands for c_____ (28⇩), i_____ (5⇩) and *freight*.

• Goods sent by air are called a_____ (31⇩). Goods sent by sea are called s_____ (33⇨).

• *FOB* stand for *free on b_____* (2⇩). It refers to the price a buyer pays a seller for goods. The price includes all the seller's costs until the goods are on the ship, plane, etc, for transportation.

• Import d_____ (11⇩) – also sometimes called an import l_____ (19⇨) – is a tax which has to be paid on goods coming into a country. A customs t_____ (27⇩) is a list of those taxes that must be paid.

• A person or company which arranges shipping and c_____ (29 ⇨) documents is called a f_____ (13⇩) agent.

• If tax on imported goods is not paid, those goods may be i_____ (30⇨) (in other words, they are kept in a secure w_____ (6⇨) at or near the p_____ (18⇨) of entry until that tax is paid).

• A c_____ (21⇨) agent arranges the import and delivery of goods at their port of d_____ (10⇨).

• As soon as goods are allowed into a country by the customs officer, we can say that they have been c_____ (1⇩).

• A record of the international trading position of a country in m_____ (34⇨) (= goods), excluding invisible trade, is called the *b_____* (22⇩) *of trade*.

• A w_____ (4⇨) price is a price paid by customers (for example, shops) who buy goods in large quantities. They sell these goods to individual customers (for example, shoppers) at a higher price which is called the r_____ (7⇩) price. Some offer d_____ (17⇨) to their customers, which means they pay a little less.

• A l_____ (25⇩) agreement allows a company to market or produce goods or services owned by another company, and is a popular means for a company to penetrate the overseas market.

For reference see *Dictionary of Business - 4th edition* (A&C Black Publishers Ltd, 978-0-713-67918-2)

- A q_____ (35⇨) is a limited amount of a good that can be brought into a country (usually as an incentive for people to buy home-produced versions of that good). This is an example of a trade b_____ (12⇩).

- When goods are sold within one country, they are transported to their place of sale by a d_____ (8⇩).

For reference see *Dictionary of Business - 4th edition* (A&C Black Publishers Ltd, 978-0-713-67918-2)

Exercise 1: Choose the best word(s) or expression(s) to complete these sentences. In some cases, more than one option is possible.

1. (At the airport. A check-in assistant is talking to a passenger) I'm afraid your flight has been **cancelled / delayed / crashed / double-booked**. It won't be leaving for another two hours.

2. (At the airport. An angry passenger is talking to her colleague) I don't believe it. The airline has **diverted / overbooked / rerouted / postponed** our flight and have told me there are no more seats available for us. We'll have to wait for the next one.

3. (A business executive is explaining why he prefers to fly business class) Flying business class is much more expensive than flying **tourist / coach / economy / club** class, but it's much more comfortable and the food is better.

4. (An announcement is being made at a port) The ship will soon be ready for **embarkation / boarding / disembarkation / climbing**. Would passengers please ensure they have their tickets ready.

5. (At the airport, an announcement is being made to passengers arriving on a flight) Welcome to London Heathrow Airport. Could we remind **transition / transitive / transitory / transit** passengers to wait in the lounge until their next flight is ready.

6. (At the airport, an urgent announcement is being made over the PA system) Would the last remaining passenger for flight BZ112 to Thessalonica please proceed immediately to **door / entrance / gate / pier** 22, where their flight is about to depart.

7. (A travel agent is telling a traveller about his flight) Your flight to Istanbul is **one way / indirect / direct / non-stop**, so you won't be landing anywhere else en route.

8. (At the airport, an assistant is helping a passenger to find the right terminal for her flight from London to Belfast) Terminals 2 and 3 are the terminals for international flights. You need terminal 1 for **domesticated / domestic / domesticity / domicile** flights.

9. (At the station, an information desk assistant is explaining ticket prices to a passenger who wants to visit a town and return on the same day). A **single / simple / one way / one direction** ticket to Bradford costs £27.50. A **return trip / round-trip / circle-trip / square-trip** ticket will cost you £42.

10. (At the bank, a clerk is telling a customer why he can't take out any more money with his American Express card). I'm really sorry, sir, but you have already exceeded your **profit margin / loyalty points / credit limit / commission rates**.

11. (On an aircraft, the captain is talking to his passengers) If you need anything during the flight, please do not hesitate to ask one of our cabin **staff / gang / team / crew** members.

12. (A radio announcement is being made for people travelling to a city for their job) Bad news for **expatriates / commuters / immigrants / migrants**, I'm afraid. Traffic on the M25 is backed up for12 miles at junction 9.

13. (An article in a magazine is talking about air travel) In a recent survey, Albion International Air Ltd was voted the world's favourite **carrier / airline / airliner / airways** for its punctuality, comfort, quality of in-flight catering and of course its standards of safety.

14. (A travel agent is explaining insurance policies to a customer) We advise you to take out our **comprehensive / adhesive / apprehensive / defensive** insurance policy which will cover you against all risks that are likely to happen.

15. (A car hire clerk is helping a customer choose a vehicle) The roads here are so bad and so full of holes that we very much recommend you hire a / an **MPV / saloon / 4x4 / van**.

For reference see *Dictionary of Business - 4th edition* (A&C Black Publishers Ltd, 978-0-713-67918-2)

Exercise 2: Choose the best word or expression from each pair in **bold** to complete this text. In some cases, both words / expressions are possible.

There are a few things that the well-prepared business traveller should sort out before they leave the country. First of all, they will need to prepare a / an (1) **schedule / itinerary** so that they know exactly where they will be and who they will seeing at various times on their (2) **voyage / trip**. Next, they should check their passport: have they got one, for a start, and is it still (3) **validated / valid**? Most countries will not let them in if their passport (4) **runs out / expires** within six months. Secondly, what about a (5) **visa / visor**? More and more countries require foreign visitors to have one, and this will cost money (and time and effort, too: in some cases, the traveller has to present himself or herself in person at the country's (6) **emmbassy / embassy**). Thirdly, they will need to get (7) **traveller's cheques / traveling cheques** and / or foreign (8) **currancy / currency**: if they choose the latter, they need to check the (9) **exchange / changing** rate to make sure they are getting a favourable (10) **deal / bargain**, and then in most cases they will need to pay (11) **comission / commission / commision** to the bank who supplies it. Finally, they should check that they have (12) **insurence / insurance / insureance** cover, that their (13) **vaccinations / vaccinnations / vacinations** are up to date, and that their mobile phone will work abroad (and if necessary, make arrangements with their (14) **provider / provisor** to ensure they can get connected to the (15) **network / website** when they arrive).

Exercise 3: Now try this quiz.

1. In which places would you *check in*?
2. You are told that you need to pay an *excess baggage* charge. What does this mean?
3. At the airport you are told you have been *bumped* from your flight. What does this mean?
4. You want an *upgrade* on your flight. What exactly do you want?
5. The flight you have booked includes free *transfers*. What are these?
6. You are travelling from Greece to the UK. Are you allowed a *duty free allowance*?
7. What is the correct word in bold in this question: 'How much is the business class **fee / fare** from Washington to Rome?'
8. What is an *e-ticket*?
9. You are flying from Cape Town to London. Would you expect to suffer *jet lag*?
10. In a hotel, what is the difference between *full-board*, *half-board* and *bed and breakfast* accommodation?
11. In a hotel, what is the difference between a *single room*, a *twin room*, a *double room* and a *suite*?
12. The hotel you want to stay at insists on charging you the *rack rate*. What is this?
13. You are in your room in a large international hotel. Which department would you call if you wanted the following?
    (a) someone to clean your room, bring you some towels and wash your shirts
    (b) to make a general enquiry
    (c) to report an electrical or plumbing problem
    (d) to help you make a national or international phone call
    (e) to have some food brought to your room
    (f) to order a taxi or have your luggage taken from or to your room
14. Rearrange the letters in bold to make the names of things you might find in a hotel room (in addition to a bed, of course).
    rwoarbed   feas   niim rab   nlboyac   ari tincnoniogdi   ate dan fceeof fteiliacis   nteelntr scesac   nori   snioleitev   oemrte ontolcr
15. The room in your hotel was *pokey*, *scruffy* and *draughty*, the hotel staff were *discourteous*, *officious* and *surly*, and the hotel food was *greasy*, *unappetising* and *repetitive*. Would you stay at the hotel again?
16. In which situations would you expect to *leave a tip*?

For reference see *Dictionary of Business - 4th edition* (A&C Black Publishers Ltd, 978-0-713-67918-2)

The four words in each set 1 - 28 below can be used with one other word (i.e., they *collocate* with that word). What is that word in each set? Choose your answers from the box. The first one has been done for you. Note that each word you choose from the box must work with *all four words* in the set.

brand	business	career	contract	corporate	cost	customer
employment	group	health	income	industrial	insurance	job	labour
management	market	minimum	~~pension~~	personal	price	private
salary	sales	shift	staff	strike	tax	

1. • _pension_ scheme • _pension_ contributions • occupational _pension_ • portable _pension_
2. • _____ address • _____ cycle • _____ expenses • _____ plan
3. • _____ application • _____ description • _____ opportunities • _____ rotation
4. • _____ freeze • _____ war • _____ fixing • _____ ceiling
5. • _____ climate • _____ culture • _____ governance • _____ image
6. • _____ accounting • _____ analysis • _____ factor • marginal _____
7. • _____ allowance • _____ bracket • _____ exemption • _____ threshold
8. • _____ accident • _____ action • _____ relations • _____ tribunal
9. • _____ age • _____ pay • _____ wage • _____ salary
10. • _____ review • _____ structure • annual _____ • basic _____
11. • _____ call • _____ notice • unofficial _____ • wildcat _____
12. • _____ transfer • _____ work • night _____ • day _____
13. • _____ audit • _____ committee • _____ style • _____ trainee
14. • _____ cover • _____ screening • _____ insurance • _____ report
15. • _____ force • _____ dispute • skilled _____ • manual _____
16. • _____ agency • _____ law • full-time _____ • temporary _____
17. • _____ policy • _____ cover • _____ broker • national _____
18. • _____ expectations • _____ ladder • _____ opportunities • _____ path
19. • _____ leader • _____ penetration • _____ research • _____ value
20. • _____ tax • _____ support • earned _____ • net _____
21. • _____ complaint • _____ expectation • _____ satisfaction • _____ service
22. • _____ enterprise • _____ ownership • _____ secretary • _____ sector
23. • _____ agency • _____ appointment • senior _____ • skeleton _____
24. • _____ discussion • _____ dynamics • _____ interview • focus _____
25. • _____ work • _____ law • _____ hire • fixed-term _____
26. • _____ analysis • _____ campaign • _____ representative • _____ team
27. • _____ allowance • _____ assistant • _____ contract • _____ development
28. • _____ leader • _____ loyalty • _____ image • own _____

For reference see *Dictionary of Business - 4th edition* (A&C Black Publishers Ltd, 978-0-713-67918-2)

Working hours and time off work

Exercise 1: Complete sentences 1 – 26 with words and expressions from the box. Note that some of the sentences refer to *shift work* (when employees work for a period and then are replaced by others). Other sentences refer to *flexible* work systems, where employees can start or stop work at different hours of the day, provided they work a certain number of hours a day or week.

allowed time	clock off	core time	double time	fixed hours
Flexible Work Regulations	flexileader	flexilagger	flexitime	full-time
graveyard shift	homeworking	job rotation	job-share	overtime	part-time
roster	rotating shifts	shift differentials	shift transfer	time and a half
time-keeping	time sheet	twilight shift	unsocial hours	work-life balance

1.   _____ is the fact of being on time for work (for example, *'He was reprimanded for bad _____'*).

2.   _____ is paid time which the management agrees an employee can spend on rest, cleaning or meals, not working.

3.   _____ is a form of employment in which two or more people do a single job or take on a specific role within a company, each person working part-time.

4.   _____ is a short form of the expression *flexible time*.

5.   A company or organisation that puts a lot of emphasis on flexibility in its employment practices is known informally as a _____.

6.   A company or organisation that puts too little emphasis on flexibility in its working practices is known informally as a _____.

7.   An employee who works _____ works at times such as in the evening, at night or during public holidays when most people are not at work.

8.   Employees who work _____ work for the normal working time (i.e. about 8 hours a day 5 days a week).

9.   Employees who work _____ do not work for the whole working week (for example, they might only work 4 hours a day instead of 8).

10.   A time for which work is paid at twice the normal rate (for example, at weekends or on public holidays) is called _____.

11.   _____ is the normal rate of pay plus 50% extra (for example, when an employee does overtime or works evenings).

12.   Hours worked more than the normal working hours are called _____.

13.   _____ is a period when employees working under a flexible time system must be present at work.

14.   The act of changing an employee's shift or working hours is called _____.

15   If a company does not operate a flexible time system, we say that the employees work _____ hours.

16.   _____ refers to a system where employees take turns in working different shifts.

17.   The _____ is an informal expression for the night shift.

18.   _____ is a working method where employees work at home (usually on computer terminals), and send the finished material back to the office by email.

For reference see *Dictionary of Business - 4th edition* (A&C Black Publishers Ltd, 978-0-713-67918-2)

19. A *duty* _____ is a list of times showing when each employee is on duty at those times.

20. When you record the time you leave work by putting a card into a special machine, you _____.

21. A _____ is a record of when employees arrive at and leave work, or one which shows how much time an employee spends on different jobs each day.

22. In Britain, parents who have children under 6, or disabled children under 18, have a legal right to have their working hours arranged to help them with their responsibilities. This right is known as _____.

23. The ability to devote a sensible amount of time to doing your job, making sure that you have enough time left over to do other things (for example, spend time with your family) is referred to as _____.

24. _____ are payments made to an employee in addition to their basic pay to compensate them for the inconvenience of the pattern of shift work.

25. The _____ is another name for the evening shift, just before it gets dark.

26. When an employee is moved systematically from one job to another, this is known as _____.

Exercise 2: Complete these sentences with an appropriate word or words, and write these words in the grid on the next page. If you do this correctly, you will reveal a hidden expression in the shaded vertical strip which means *time off work granted to an employee to deal with personal or family problems*. Some of the letters have already been put into the grid to help you.

Several of the sentences use the word *leave*. In these cases, *leave* is a noun for *permission to be away from work* (e.g., 'He isn't here, he's on leave'). Employees can *be* or *go on leave*.

1. A certificate from a doctor to show that an employee has been ill is called a _____ *certificate*.

2. A holiday from work which is fixed by law is called a _____ *holiday*.

3. A period when a woman is away from work to have a baby (but is still paid) is called _____ *leave*.

4. Leave during which an employee receives no money is called _____ leave.

5. A period of leave during which an employee is not allowed into the company offices is known informally as _____ leave.

6. A period of paid or unpaid time off work for the purposes of research, study or travel is called a _____.

7. The percentage of a workforce which is away from work with no good excuse is called the _____ rate.

8. A day when all employees in the country are allowed to take a day off work is called a _____ _____.

9. A period of paid leave given by some companies to staff who have completed several years of service is called _____-_____ leave.

10. A person's right to something (for example, their right to a paid holiday from work) is called an _____.

For reference see *Dictionary of Business - 4th edition* (A&C Black Publishers Ltd, 978-0-713-67918-2)

11. If an employee is away from work without permission and without a good reason, we can say that s/he has taken _____ *absence from work*.

12. When an employee is sick and has to wait three days before s/he can claim sick pay, these days are known as _____ *days*.

13. If an employee has permission to be away from work, s/he has *leave of* _____.

14. When an employee gets time off from work instead of pay (for example, if they work overtime and get some time off work instead of overtime pay), we say that they take *time off* _____ _____.

15. A short period of leave given to a father to be away from work when his partner has a baby is called _____ *leave*.

16. Paid time off from work given to an employee to help him / her deal with personal affairs is called _____ *leave*.

17. A holiday or period when people are not working is called a _____ (especially in the USA).

18. A payment made by the government or by a private insurance company to someone who is ill and cannot work is called *sickness* _____.

#												
1.			D				L					
2.	T		T									
3.						T		R				Y
4.			U				D					
5.			G				E			N		
6.					A	B					C	
7.			A		S			E		I		
8.		U					O				A	
9.					O		G		R			C
10.					T					M		
11.			U				H				S	
12.		A	I									
13.						N	E					

#								
14.					I	E		
15.		P					T	
16.					A	S		
17.						C	T	
18.				B			F	

For reference see *Dictionary of Business - 4th edition* (A&C Black Publishers Ltd, 978-0-713-67918-2)

Exercise 1: In the following sentences and paragraphs, one of the words in each of the word pairs in **bold** is wrong and one is right. Identify the most appropriate word in each case. You will find this easier to do if you read each paragraph through first so that you have a better idea of what it is about (Note that the wrong words are real English words, but do not fit into the context of the sentence / paragraph).

Paragraph (A)

If there is a (1) **despite / dispute** between the management and the union in a company which cannot be (2) **restored / resolved,** and as a result a (3) **strike / stroke** looks likely, a third party might be called in to (4) **abdicate / arbitrate**.

Paragraph (B)

Three managers have been accused of (1) **fraught / fraud**, (2) **dissemination / discrimination**, (3) **bullying / bumbling**, (4) **racy / racial** (5) **obtuse / abuse** and (6) **sectional / sexual** (7) **harassment / arrestment** . As a result two of them have been (8) **fried / fired** and one has been (9) **suspected / suspended** without pay. The first two are claiming (10) **unfair / unfaithful** (11) **dismissive / dismissal** and plan to (12) **appeal / appal**. The third has applied for a job with the government.

Paragraph (C)

We would like to point out that there have been several (1) **breaches / beaches** of the company's 'No smoking' policy. We also have proof that several factory floor workers have been (2) **neglecting / negotiating** their duties, and there have also been several incidences of (3) **insurrection / insubordination** towards senior managers and intentional (4) **damning / damage** of company property. If this happens again, those responsible will be taken before a (5) **disconcerting / disciplinary** (6) **broad / board** and could face (7) **instant / instance** (8) **dismal / dismissal**. We would like to stress that the company has a (9) **nil-tolerant / zero tolerance** policy towards those who misbehave or break the rules.

Paragraph (D)

The management are fully aware that because of staff (1) **shortness / shortages** we are all (2) **overstretched / oversubscribed** at the moment, Mr Harrington, but we suggest that if you have a (3) **grievance / grievous**, you put it to us in writing rather than encourage your colleagues to hold a sudden (4) **walkout / walkabout**. We'd like you to treat this as a (5) **verbal / verdant** (6) **warming / warning**: the next time it happens, we will be obliged to ask for your (7) **notice / note**.

Paragraph (E)

What a terrible month! Sales have (1) **droned / dropped** by 40%, six employees have been made (2) **recumbent / redundant**, two senior managers have (3) **resigned / resided**, our main supplier has gone (4) **bankrolled / bankrupt**, someone has (5) **haggled / hacked** into the company website and given us a (6) **virus / viscous** (with the result that the entire computer system has (7) **crashed / cracked**), and the coffee machine is *still* out of (8) **odour / order**.

For reference see *Dictionary of Business - 4th edition* (A&C Black Publishers Ltd, 978-0-713-67918-2)

Paragraph (F)

One problem that many companies face is that of their employees (1) **plateauing / plating**. This often happens when there is a lack of opportunity for promotion. In such situations, employees may feel they are lacking sufficient (2) **simulation / stimulation**, and as a result could lose their (3) **motivation / motorisation** and display less (4) **indicative / initiative** than before. This in turn can lead to reduced (5) **proclivity / productivity** for the company concerned. A good manager should recognise the potential danger signs, and (6) **implement / inclement** any solutions that they think might help.

Paragraph (G)

An unhappy workforce should be easy for a good manager to spot. Basically, if staff (1) **turnover / turnaround** is high and staff (2) **detention / retention** is low, (3) **conflict / conscript** situations are frequent, there is frequent staff (4) **absenteeism / abstention**, poor (5) **timeserving / timekeeping** and (6) **misconduct / misconception** in the workplace, if (7) **moral / morale** seems generally low and if there is often the threat of (8) **industrial / industrious** action, it is time to act. The first thing to do is to (9) **counsel / council** employees and try to establish the cause of their (10) **grievances / grief**.

Exercise 2. Match the words in paragraphs A – G above with their definitions below.

1. The practice of staying away from work, often without a good reason.
2. Reaching a point where you cannot go any further in your job.
3. To give professional advice to someone on personal or professional issues.
4. The frequency within which employees people leave a job and are replaced by new employees.
5. Not needed for a job anymore.
6. A disagreement.
7. To be in a situation where you have too much to do.
8. To try to settle a disagreement between two or more people / groups.
9. The practice of treating people in different ways (because of their sex, race, religion, etc).
10. Regularly worrying or bothering someone.
11. A complaint.
12. The eagerness to work well.
13. Bad behaviour at work.
14. A failure to carry out the terms of an agreement, or the failure to follow rules.
15. The sudden stopping of work by employees when they leave their place of work because of a disagreement.
16. The decision or idea to start or do something.
17. The refusal to obey someone with more authority.
18. To ask someone formally to change a decision that you are not happy with.
19. Spoken.
20. To put something (for example, a plan) into action.
21. Official written information telling an employee that he / she is going to lose his / her job.
22. A feeling of confidence or satisfaction.

Also see *Dispute resolution* on pages 11–12.

For reference see *Dictionary of Business - 4th edition* (A&C Black Publishers Ltd, 978-0-713-67918-2)

Abbreviations (pages 1–2)

Across: **2.** European **4.** buyout **8.** selling **9.** business **11.** technological **13.** Director **14.** investment **15.** mergers **17.** earnings **19.** earn **20.** Tax **22.** opportunities **25.** Executive **26.** vitae **27.** needs **29.** time **32.** price **34.** Financial **37.** questions **38.** injury **39.** index **41.** annum (do not confuse p.a. with PA: a personal assistant) **43.** annual **45.** Commerce **49.** information **51.** product **52.** secure **54.** domestic **56.** person (the plural is *VIP's: very important people / persons*)

Down: **1.** quality **3.** parity **5.** public **6.** meeting **7.** relations **10.** credit **12.** Administration **15.** methods (or sometimes management) **16.** resources **18.** sale **21.** profit **23.** possible **24.** central **28.** delivery **30.** first **31.** Qualification **33.** national **35.** Insurance **36.** development **40.** share **42.** thousand **44.** electronic **46.** research **47.** postage **48.** Internet **50.** free **53.** you (the same pronunciation as the letter *u*) **55.** time

Appraisals, training and development (pages 3–5)

Exercise 1:
The questions in this exercise are typical questions that might be asked at an appraisal / assessment interview (sometimes informally called *job chats*).

1. standards **2.** knowledge **3.** quality **4.** objectives **5.** improvement **6.** strengths **7.** training **8.** progression **9.** schedule **10.** challenging **11.** least **12.** workload **13.** description **14.** defined **15.** advancement **16.** improving **17.** morale **18.** relationship **19.** discipline **20.** treatment **21.** promptly **22.** complaints **23.** progress **24.** praise **25.** facilities **26.** provisions **27.** recommend **28.** comments

Normally before an appraisal, employees fill in a *self-appraisal* form. Note that appraisals / assessments are normally *knowledge-based* (what the employee knows),and *performance-based* (how well the employee has worked, and the results s/he has achieved). Appraisals can be *two-way*, with the employee telling the company how s/he feels about it, and his / her role in it. A good company will always listen to the *feedback* it receives from its employees.
Performance-based appraisals often use a method known as *BARS* (*behaviourally-anchored rating scales*), where performance is based on a typical performance criteria set for each individual employee.

Many companies have adopted the practice of *360-degree appraisals*. Colleagues above, below and at the same rank as the employee being appraised are asked to contribute their views on that employee before the interview takes place.

If an employee is not performing well in his / her current position, s/he might be given a *remedial transfer*. This means that s/he is transferred to a more suitable job. The informal expression is a *turkey trot*.

Note that many of the questions in this exercise might also be asked at an exit interview, when an employee is interviewed before s/he leaves the company. The questions would normally be expressed in the past tense, e.g., Did you think...?, Were you happy...?, etc. In

addition to the questions in the exercise, exit interviews might also ask the employee how s/he felt about the rewards, benefits and services offered by the company (holiday pay, sick pay, pension scheme, health insurance, life assurance, loan facilities, educational assistance, sports and social facilities, refreshment facilities, HR services, etc).

Exercise 2:
1. continuous personal development (also called *continual personal development*) **2.** assertiveness training **3.** experiential learning (also called *learning by doing*) **4.** adventure training **5.** in-tray learning **6.** team-building (an employee who works well as part of a team is called a *team player*) **7.** carousel learning **8.** sales training **9.** modern apprenticeship **10.** an induction course **11.** off-the-job training (training which takes place on the company premises during work time is called *on-the-job training* or *in-house / in-company training*) **12.** open learning **13.** training needs analysis **14.** total quality management (TQM)

Note: a *trainer* is somebody who trains staff, a *trainee* is somebody who learns how to do something.

Here are some other words and expressions that you might find useful:
adult education   correspondence course   team learning distance learning   training needs   performance appraisal staff appraisal   individual learning   autonomous learning learning curve   learning style   evaluation and assessment work-based learning   INSET (in-service training) Investor in People (a national programme for employee development sponsored by the UK government) managerial grid

Changes (page 6–7)

Exercise 1:
1. widening **2.** sharp decline / fall **3.** general improvement **4.** expansion **5.** weakening **6.** tightening up **7.** constant rise **8.** dramatic increase **9.** steady decrease **10.** phased out **11.** build up **12.** cuts **13.** deterioration **14.** considerable growth **15.** upward trend **16.** marked progress **17.** upgrade **18.** streamline **19.** Downsizing **20.** fluctuated **21.** amended **22.** restructure

Exercise 2:
1. exchanged **2.** adapt **3.** outsourced (if you *outsource* a part of a company, you move part of the company operations from your home country to another country, or from inside your company to another company) **4.** transformed **5.** renovated **6.** switched **7.** vary **8.** expanded **9.** dissolve (we could also use the phrasal verb *break up*) **10.** revised (*revised* prices are usually increased, but they can also go down, as in the first part of this example)

Business colours (page 8)

1. (a) orange goods (= goods that are not bought as often as *fast-moving items* such as food products, but are replaced from time to time.   (b) brown goods (= electrical equipment for home entertainment).   (c) white goods (= machines that are used in the kitchen / utility room. White

Answer key

goods can also refer to household linen, such as towels and sheets). (d) yellow goods (= high-priced goods which are kept in use for a relatively long time, and so are not replaced very often). (e) red goods (= fast-selling convenience goods, especially food products).

Note that items such as televisions, stereo systems and even clothes could also be classified as yellow goods, especially if they are very expensive.

2. (d) red tape. **3.** These informal expressions refer to bank accounts**.** If an account is *in the red*, it is showing a debit or loss (e.g., less than £0). If an account is *in the black*, it is showing a profit, or (if used to refer to a company) having more assets than debt. **4.** black (we can also say *hidden economy*, *parallel economy* or *shadow economy*). **5.** Green taxes. **6.** False. A blue-chip investment is the purchase of low-risk shares in a company which is performing well. **7.** (b) to blacklist (this can also be a noun: *a blacklist*). **8.** Yes, provided it has received *planning permission* to do so. Compare *greenfield site* (= an area of land - usually in the country - that has not been built on before) with *brownfield site* (= an area of land, especially in an urban area, that had buildings on it in the past, and can be built on again). **9.** A *white-collar worker* is someone who works in an office. A *blue-collar worker* is someone who works in a factory. **10.** white-collar (see number 9 above). **11.** Women. This is an informal and rather sexist expression for a job that is normally held by a woman (especially a young one). **12.** a black market (often used in the expression *a black market economy*)**. 13.** Probably a bad thing. Blue-sky ideas (also called *blue-sky thinking*) are extremely idealistic, ambitious, unrealistic and unconventional. **14.** Unhappy: this is an informal expression for stocks and bonds that have no value. **15.** All of these.

Contracts (pages 9–10)

Exercise 1:
Here is the complete text:

A contract can be defined as 'an **agreement** between two or more parties to create legal **obligations** between them'. Some contracts are made **under seal**': in other words, they are **signed** and sealed (stamped) by the parties involved. Most contracts are made **verbally** or **in writing**. The essential elements of a contract are: (a) that an **offer** made by one party should be **accepted** by the other; (b) **consideration** (the price in money, goods or some other **reward**, paid by one party in exchange for another party agreeing to do something); (c) the **intention** to create legal relations. The **terms** of a contract may be *express* (clearly stated) or *implied* (not clearly **stated** in the contract, but generally understood)**.** A **breach** of contract by one party of their **contractual liability** entitles the other party to **sue** for **damages** or, in some cases, to seek specific performance**.** In such circumstances, the contract may be **voided** (in other words, it becomes *invalid*).

Exercise 2:
1. 1. parts = parties 2. False 3. C
2. 1. terminator = termination 2. True 3. obligated / required
3. 1. un-negotiable = non-negotiable 2. True (*amend* = *change* or *alter*. The noun is *an amendment*. You can

make an amendment) 3. oral / spoken / implied / understood
(Note that if a contract is *on paper*, it is called a *written* contract)
4. 1. in beach of = in breach of (*breach* can also be a verb: *to breach a contract*) 2. abide by (in paragraph 1) 3. False (they have only broken one of the *clauses*, or *parts*, of the contract)
5. 1. period of notification = period of notice 2. agreement 3. True
6. 1. anointment = appointment 2. False (*amalgamation* comes from the verb *to amalgamate*: to join and become one. We can also say *merger*, from the verb *to merge*) 3. False (he is not allowed to have a *controlling interest* in the company, so his ability to buy stocks is restricted) 4. None (*third parties* are people or groups other than Mr Wiley and the amalgamation of AKL Publishing and Berryhill Books)

Dispute resolution (pages 11–12)

Exercise 1:
Here is the complete text:

A *dispute* is an argument or **disagreement**. In business and commerce, there are usually two types of dispute.

The first of these is an **industrial** dispute, which is between an employer and an employer's representative, which in many cases is a **trade union**. These are usually the result of disagreements over pay, conditions of work and unfair **dismissals**, including **redundancy** (the laying-off of employees because they are not needed). The least favourable outcome of this type of dispute is usually industrial **action**, often in the form of a **strike** (where employees stop working). Alternatively, employees may stage a **go-slow** (where they work at less than their normal speed). They may also adopt a **work-to-rule** strategy, in which they strictly follow all the **terms** of their contract, and obey other **regulations** to the letter. They may also refuse to work **overtime**. The result of this is usually **decreased** productivity for the company.

The second type of dispute is a **commercial** dispute, which is a disagreement between two businesses. This is usually the result of a **breach** of contract (in which one or both sides fails to agree to, or **abide by**, the terms and **conditions** of a contract drawn up between them). In extreme cases, this may result in **litigation** (in which one side brings a **suit** against the other in a court of law), with the aim of getting financial **compensation**, or of legally obliging the other side to abide by their contractual **obligations**.

Disputes do not necessarily have to be settled in an imposed court case. **Mediation** (an attempt by a **disinterested*** third party to make two sides in an argument agree) is often quicker, more **cost-effective** and less stressful for the parties involved.

* *Disinterested* has a similar meaning to *impartial* (see exercise 2).

Exercise 2:

1. alternative **2.** litigation (the verb is *to litigate*, the adjective is *litigious*) **3.** voluntary / consent **4.** impartial / mediator (the verb is *to mediate*) **5.** facilitator **6.** joint session / caucus **7.** confidential/ disclosed **8.** resolutions / practical / beneficial **9.** negotiations **10.** settlements / compromise / mutual **11.** bound **12.** prejudice **13.** binding / honour **14.** contractually **15.** arbitration **16.** tribunal **17.** arbitrator **18.** adjudication **19.** public domain

Earnings, rewards and benefits 1 (pages 13–14)

1. wage / salary **2.** remuneration **3.** overtime **4.** increment **5.** deduction **6.** dock **7.** minimum **8.** double time **9.** time and a half **10.** pension plan **11.** rise (we can also say *raise*) **12.** advance / sub **13.** payslip **14.** bonus **15.** payroll **16.** package **17.** weighting (for example, a job advertisement might offer an annual salary of £30,000 + £4,000 London *weighting*) **18.** leave entitlement **19.** Income / expenditure **20.** stock options (we can also say *share options*. Some companies have something called an *ESOP*: an *employee share ownership plan*) **21.** incentive plans **22.** rate **23.** redundancy pay **24.** discount **25.** relocation allowance **26.** danger **27.** gross **28.** net (also called *take-home pay*) **29.** index-linked **30.** commensurate (for example, *Your salary will be commensurate with your experience and qualifications*) **31.** arrears **32.** direct deposit **33.** performance related **34.** golden handshake (some companies also give new employees a *golden hello* when they accept a job with the company, and some companies may offer new employees a *golden parachute*, which guarantees them a special payment if they are *made redundant*)

Earnings, rewards and benefits 2 (page 15)

1. direct / extrinsic **2.** extrinsic / direct **3.** basic **4.** performance-related **5.** commissions **6.** recognition **7.** Gainsharing **8.** motivation **9.** production bonus **10.** premium bonus **11.** attendance bonus **12.** acceptance bonus (informally called a *golden hello*) **13.** Profit sharing **14.** benefits **15.** extras **16.** pensions **17.** share **18.** insurance **19.** duvet days **20.** fixed **21.** flexible (also known as a *cafeteria-style benefits plan*) **22.** Incentive **23.** indirect / intrinsic **24.** intrinsic / indirect **25.** status **26.** satisfaction **27.** growth / development **28.** skill **29.** development **30.** security **31.** comradeship

Here are some other words and expressions that you might find useful:

salaried (the adjective of *salary*)   earnings   real earnings   take-home pay   well-paid   low-paid   pay packet   pension contributions   accrual rate   hourly / daily rate   occupational / company pension (scheme)   remuneration   portable pension (scheme)   per day / per diem   perks   increments a year / per annum   wage / salary review   on-target earnings   parity   to erode wage differentials   incentive   basic / flat rate   reward management   broadbanding   compensation package   benefit in kind   reward review   exploding bonus   health insurance   holiday pay   sick pay   life assurance

Formal words (pages 16–17)

Exercise 1:
1. analyse (spelt *analyze* in American English) **2.** assessed at **3.** averting **4.** administer **5.** assigned **6.** annulled **7.** audit **8.** appealed to **9.** addressed **10.** award **11.** admonished **12.** awaiting **13.** adjusted **14.** adjourned **15.** appointed

Exercise 2:
1. attend **2.** advised **3.** assist **4.** amalgamated **5.** attempt **6.** assured **7.** sequestered (we can also say *sequestrated*) **8.** settle **9.** tender **10.** dismissed **11.** engage (we can also say *employ*, *recruit* or *hire*) **12.** waived **13.** present **14.** elected **15.** licensed

Exercise 3:
1. retain **2.** specify **3.** redeployed **4.** consulted **5.** undertaken **6.** reinstated **7.** inquiring (note that in this sentence, *inquiring* must be followed by *into*: 'We are *inquiring into* the background of the new supplier'. *Inquiring* can also be written *enquiring*) **8.** consented **9.** notified **10.** briefed **11.** outlined **12.** upgraded

The word in the shaded vertical strip (and the one that can be used to replace the words in **bold** in number 13) is **apportioning**.

Business idioms (page 18–19)

Exercise 1:
1. goes belly up **2.** rat race **3.** turkey trot **4.** a people churner **5.** an ohnosecond **6.** a dogsbody **7.** a sickie **8.** work rage (also called *desk rage* when applied to people working in an office) **9.** out of the loop **10.** a cushy number **11.** got the boot **12.** pencil-whip **13.** a helicopter view **14.** eye service **15.** a mushroom job **16.** a Mickey Mouse job **17.** swinging the lead **18.** a lemon

Exercise 2:
1. stress puppy (= someone who seems to enjoy being under pressure, but still complains about it) **2.** shape up or ship out (= improve or leave) **3.** empty suit (= someone - usually in a fairly high position - who doesn't really contribute very much to a company or organisation) **4.** kiss up to (= to be very nice and polite to someone in a position of power. It is a negative expression. We can also say *schmooze up to* or *suck up to*) **5.** dead wood (= the employees who are losing a company money. We can use the expression *to cut out the dead wood* in this context) **6.** glad hand (= to shake hands with people. We can also use the expression *press the flesh*) **7.** seagull manager (= someone who is brought in to a company to deal with a problem or make changes, achieves nothing, annoys everyone and then leaves) **8.** ear candy (= kind words of praise and encouragement) **9.** wombat (an acronym: *waste of money, brains and time*. *Basket case* - see number 14. below - could also be used in this sentence if speaker B is talking about the boss) **10.** dumbsizing (= to dismiss the best workers in a company. It is an adaptation of the word *downsizing*. If a company dismisses those workers who do <u>not</u> contribute much and are losing the company money, we could say that they *smartsize*) **11.** happy camper (= someone who enjoys their job, although the expression is often used ironically) **12.** wiggle room (= time to think before making an important decision) **13.** busymeet (= a business meeting) **14.** basket case (= a company or a person who is in such bad condition that they are beyond help) **15.** trim the fat (= dismiss / lay off of those employees who do not work well or are *surplus to requirement*) **16.** cash cow (= a product or service that makes a lot of money with a minimum amount of advertising)

Answer key

IT and e-commerce (pages 20-22)

Exercise 1:

1. desktop **2.** laptop (also sometimes called a *notebook*)
3. components **4.** CPU **5.** hard drive **6.** hard disk
7. memory **8.** software **9.** word processing
10. spreadsheet **11.** DTP **12.** load (we can also say
install) **13.** CD / DVD drive **14.** USB port **15.** memory
stick **16.** monitor **17.** keyboard **18.** printer **19.** scanner
20. mouse **21.** Internet (sometimes called the *World
Wide Web*) **22.** provider (also called an *Internet Service
provider*, or *ISP*) **23.** browser **24.** download **25.** chatrooms
26. newsgroups **27.** website **28.** log on **29.** pop-up
30. search engine **31.** keywords **32.** links (also called
hyperlinks or *hypertext links*) **33.** domain (name)
34. homepage **35.** on-line **36.** log out (we can also say
log off) **37.** bookmark **38.** email **39.** password (most
email providers also ask their subscribers to enter a
username, which is similar to a password) **40.** spam
41. delete **42.** attachment **43.** virus **44.** crashing
45. anti-virus software **46.** update (it)

Exercise 2:

1. A JPEG is a method of reducing, or *compressing*,
computer files that contain images so that they can be
sent quickly by email over the Internet (it is also the name
of a file that is produced by this method) **2.** A *file* is a set
of information or a *document* that is stored under a
particular name on a computer, a *folder* is a group of
related programs or documents stored together on a
computer **3.** *Freeware* is free software available on the
Internet, *shareware* is similar, but users are asked to make
a voluntary monetary contribution for its use, or are
encouraged to buy a more advanced version **4.** *Spyware*
is computer software that secretly records the websites
you visit on your computer, and this information is then
used by companies who try to sell you things **5.** The
Internet is a computer system, or network, that allows
people in different parts of the world to exchange
information (using websites and sending emails, etc). An
intranet is a computer network that can only be used
within a company or organisation. An *extranet* is similar to
an intranet, but also allows access by others associated
with that company or organisation (for example,
suppliers, buyers, etc) **6.** She has finished shopping and
is now going to pay **7.** (a) The user 'signs' the contract
by clicking on a box or boxes to show that he / she agrees
with the *terms and conditions* **8.** Internet Service
Provider **9.** (b) **10.** (c) (A company that only does
business on the Internet is called a *dot.com business*. A
company that does not have an Internet shopping facility
is known as a *bricks and mortar business*) **11.** Frequently
asked questions **12.** (a) **13.** Business to business
14. An *auto response* **15.** (b) UCE = *unsolicited
commercial email* **16.** *Broadband* is a class of
transmission system that allows large amounts of data to
be transferred at high speed over the Internet; an *ISDN
line* is a digital telephone network that supports advanced
communication services and can be used for high-speed
data transmission **17.** (b) **18.** personal identification
number, a private code number that only the user knows
(also required when using a credit / debit card in a cash
machine or in a shop) **19.** They are forms of on-screen
advertising **20.** No. An *anti-site*, also called a *hate-site* or
gripe-site, is a website set up by an unhappy (ex-)
customer so that they can publicly say bad things about
your company, and encourage other people to do the
same **21.** A *hacker* is someone who uses a computer to
connect to other people's computers secretly and often

illegally, so that they can find or change information. The
verb is *to hack* **22.** A *firewall* protects your computer or
network, or certain files and folders on that computer /
network, from being illegally accessed by a *hacker* (see
number 21 above) **23.** If a company is *Amazoned*, is has
lost a large share of its market to a competitor because it
has failed to develop an effective business strategy
(especially if it has failed to utilise IT technology). This is an
informal word, named after the Internet company
Amazon.com, who very quickly took a large share of the
book market before expanding into other areas **24.** (e)
Also called a *heavy site*. This is an informal expression
25. Phishing (pronounced like *fishing*) is an informal word
which refers to sending emails that are designed to trick
people into giving away personal information, such as
bank account details. This information is then used to
steal from those people. More advanced *phishers* set up
bogus websites that look like real websites (especially
ones that look like bank websites) that try to trick the
unwary or gullible **26.** You would probably feel rather
unhappy, especially if you were the company's *website
manager*: a *cobweb site* is a website that contains a lot of
out-of-date information, and if it looks like an *angry fruit
salad*, it has an interface that is particularly unattractive to
look at **27.** *Spider food* is an informal expression that
refers to words that are embedded in a web page to
attract search engines. As a result, your website would
receive a lot of visitors **28.** You are if you were able to
answer most of the questions in this exercise: someone
who is *buzzword compliant* is familiar with the latest
computer and IT terms and expressions. It is an informal
expression.

Jobs and positions (pages 23–24)

Exercise 1:

1. Receptionist **2.** Human Resources Manager **3.** Secretary
4. Girl Friday (this is rather a sexist expression)
5. Technical Support Consultant **6.** Company Director
7. Managing Director **8.** Chief Executive Officer **9.** Personal
Assistant **10.** Company Secretary **11.** Chairman
12. Non-executive Director **13.** Production Manager
14. Assistant Manager **15.** Trainer

Exercise 2:

1. Accountant **2.** External Auditor **3.** Area Manager
4. Marketing Manager **5.** Advertising Manager **6.** Sales
Representative (often shortened to *rep*) **7.** Foreman
8. Trade Union Representative **9.** Official Mediator
10. Arbitrator **11.** Graduate Trainee **12.** IT Consultant
13. Telesales Manager **14.** Official receiver **15.** Security
Guard

Letters (pages 25–27)

(A): 6, 22, 46, 47, 56 **(B)**: 5, 21, 35, 39, 40 **(C)**: 3, 17,
34, 41, 52 **(D)**: 7, 16, 37, 43, 49 **(E)**: 13 (this could also
fit in F), 33, 38, 48, 51 **(F)**: 2, 9, 23, 29, 59 **(G)**: 1, 8,
25 (this could also fit in H), 26, 60 **(H)**: 4, 12, 27, 42, 54
(I): 10, 24, 32, 36, 55 **(J)**: 11, 14, 30, 45, 58 **(K)**: 15,
18, 28, 44, 53

The following extracts do not match any of the letter types
in the box:

19 (a reminder from a company to a client to pay them),
20 (a letter or email reserving a hotel room), **31** (a letter or
email requesting something), **50** (a covering letter or note

sent with a catalogue and price list), **57** (an order from a client for some products).

> Usage notes:
> • Begin all letters with *Dear* + the recipient's family name (if you know it), or with *Dear Sir / Madam* if you don't.
> • If you are not sure if a woman is married or single, begin it *Dear Ms* + her family name (this is now the accepted form of address even if you *do* know whether she is married or not).
> • Letters that begin with a name (e.g., *Dear Mr Brown*, *Dear Ms Smith*) end with *Yours sincerely*. Letters that begin with *Dear Sir / Madam* end with *Yours faithfully*.
> • Use the active rather than the passive voice (for example, instead of "*Your order has been received*", write "*We have received your order*". Instead of "*With reference to…*", write "*I refer to…*", etc).
> • Ordinal numbers (for dates, e.g., the *first* of November, the *seventh* of April) are sometimes followed by letters (e.g., *1st* November, *7th* April), but this is less common now than it used to be. *1* November, *7* April, etc, is more common.
> • You should avoid using abbreviated dates (e.g., *12/11/05*) in business letters.
> • Note that modern business letters should be brief. The message you want to communicate should be done in the most economical way, while remaining clear and polite (remember this acronym: KISS - **K**eep **i**t **s**hort and **s**imple)

Meetings and presentations (page 28)

1. open **2.** welcoming **3.** participants **4.** attendance **5.** supporting **6.** agenda **7.** progress **8.** schedule **9.** get through **10.** achieve **11.** goals **12.** objectives **13.** chair (we can also say *preside over*) **14.** contribute **15.** clarification **16.** interrupt **17.** issues **18.** address (= *discuss/talk about*) **19.** bringing up **20.** matters **21.** priority **22.** summarizing **23.** points **24.** recommendations **25.** open floor **26.** opinions **27.** closes **28.** notes **29.** minutes **30.** report **31.** complaints **32.** questions **33.** floor **34.** discuss **35.** conference **36.** venue **37.** speakers **38.** presentations **39.** delegates **40.** contingency **41.** implement

Money and finance (pages 29–30)

Exercise 1:
1. lend / borrow **2.** credit / debit **3.** insolvent / bankrupt **4.** dividend / royalty **5.** shares / stocks **6.** gross / net **7.** deposit / withdraw **8.** tax /duty **9.** income / expenditure **10.** overpriced / exorbitant **11.** wage / salary **12.** invoice / receipt **13.** discount / refund **14.** refund / rebate **15.** inflation / deflation **16.** pension / redundancy pay **17.** statement / balance **18.** commission / interest **19.** compound / simple **20.** working capital / venture capital **21.** fund / underwrite **22.** audit / budget **23.** subsidize / sponsor (or fund) **24.** honour / default

Note that many of the words in this exercise can be used in other ways. For example, the verb *deposit* in number 7 can also be a noun (a *deposit*), and the verb *withdraw* can be made into a noun (a *withdrawal*).

Exercise 2:
1. Business overheads **2.** Credit risk **3.** Pension plan **4.** Profit margin **5.** Exchange rate **6.** Cash flow **7.** Credit limit **8.** Capital gains **9.** Down payment **10.** Risk management **11.** Money laundering **12.** Offshore banking **13.** Foreign currency **14.** Value added tax **15.** Net operating income **16.** Operating profit **17.** Interest rate **18.** Budgetary constraints **19.** Finance company **20.** Expense account **21.** Return on investment **22.** Rate of return **23.** Real assets **24.** Dynamic pricing **25.** Management buyout **26.** Budget deficit **27.** Consumer spending **28.** Income tax **29.** Golden handshake **30.** Price insensitive

Numbers and symbols (page 31)

1. 2006 = two thousand and six (some people also say *twenty oh six*) / 1994 = nineteen ninety four **2.** 24/7 = twenty four seven (= 24 hours a day, 7 days a week) **3.** 8.4% = eight point four per cent **4.** 3.45 = three forty five, or quarter to four **5.** 1800 = eighteen hundred (hours) **6.** 30 June = the thirtieth of June *or* June the thirtieth **7.** 10/3/07 = the tenth of March two thousand and seven (in the UK) or the third of October two thousand and seven (in the USA). Alternatively, you could say *the tenth of the third oh seven* **8.** 27½ = twenty seven and a half **9.** ¾ = three quarters **10.** 2m x 1m x 1m = two metres by one metre by one metre **11.** £10.99 = ten pounds ninety nine (or *ten pounds and ninety nine pence**) **12.** £100.99 = one hundred pounds ninety nine (or *one hundred pounds and ninety nine pence*) **13.** £120.75 = one hundred and twenty pounds seventy five (or *one hundred and twenty pounds and seventy five pence*) / £1120.75 = One thousand, one hundred and twenty pounds seventy five (or *one thousand, one hundred and twenty pounds and seventy five pence*) **14.** ACB81 - 25/B = ACB eighty one dash (or *hyphen*) 25 slash (or *stroke*) B **15.** 020 7921 3567 = oh two oh, seven nine two one, three five six seven **16.** 0845 601 5884 = oh eight four five, six oh one, five double eight four **17.** 0800 231415 = oh eight hundred, two three one four one five (or oh eight hundred, twenty three, fourteen, fifteen)** **18.** 999 = nine nine nine / 911 = nine one one **19.** # = hash / 0 = zero / * = star **20.** £200K = two hundred thousand pounds / mid-50's = mid-fifties **21.** $6M = six million dollars **22.** M25 = M twenty five / M4 = M four / A329 = A three two nine (these are British road classifications. M = motorway. A = main road) **23.** 2:1 = two to one (when talking about odds and ratios) **24.** @snailmail.co.uk = at snailmail dot co dot u k **25.** GR8 = great / :-) = happy / CUL8R = see you later (informal abbreviations and emoticons*** such as these are commonly used in text messages, notes and email) **26.** 4x4 = four by four (a vehicle with four-wheel drive, also called a *4WD*) **27.** 2:0 = two nil / 3:3 = three all **28.** 37,762,418 = thirty seven million, seven hundred and sixty two thousand, four hundred and eighteen **29.** © = copyright (the material cannot be copied without permission) **30.** ® = registered (the name is registered, and cannot be used by another company for another product)

* The British currency, called *sterling*, consists of pounds (£) and pence (p). £1 = 100p. Some people say *pee* instead of *pence*, but many people dislike this.

** For more information on how to say telephone numbers, see the information in the answer key for *Telephoning*.

*** :-) is an *emoticon*, a symbol that shows emotion. Emoticons take the form of a face on its side, and use standard punctuation symbols and letters. In this case, it is

Answer key

a smiling face to show happiness. Other emoticons include **:-(** to show unhappiness, **:-0** to show surprise, **:-||** to show anger, **:-@** to show fear, **:-X** to indicate a kiss. Some computers automatically turn some emoticons into proper faces (for example, by entering **:-)** , the computer automatically makes a ☺).

Phrasal verbs 1 (pages 32–34)

1. ⇩: run with **2.** ⇨: fighting against **3.** ⇩: get across **4.** ⇨: turned down **5.** ⇨: stand off **6.** ⇩: find out **7.** ⇨: give up **8.** ⇩: phased in **9.** ⇨: carry on **10.** ⇨: hand over **11.** ⇩: give in **12.** ⇨: called off **13.** ⇩: standing in **14.** ⇩: held down **15.** ⇨: build into **16.** ⇩: broken up **17.** ⇨: bring down **17.** ⇩: bring out **18.** ⇨: held back **19.** ⇨: fill in **20.** ⇨: broke down **20.** ⇩: brought up **21.** ⇨: gearing up **22.** ⇩: cut down **23.** ⇨: burn out **24.** ⇩: backed out **25.** ⇩: took up **26.** ⇩: held up **27.** ⇨: got on **28.** ⇩: carry out **29.** ⇩: get back **30.** ⇩: got out **31.** ⇨: get ahead **32.** ⇨: put off **33.** ⇨: put out **34.** ⇨: opt out **35.** ⇩: take on **36.** ⇨: cancelled out **37.** ⇨: fallen behind

Note that some of the phrasal verbs in this exercise actually use *two* particles. For example: to *cut down on* something. The second particle appears in the sentence and has not been included in the crossword grid.

Phrasal verbs 2 (page 35)

There are a few possible matches, but these are the best options
1. F **2.** M **3.** R **4.** T **5.** L **6.** A **7.** G **8.** N **9.** Q **10.** C **11.** J **12.** S **13.** H **14.** I **15.** P **16.** O **17.** E **18.** D **19.** K **20.** B

Production and operations (pages 36–38)

Exercise 1:
1. lead time (also called *cycle time*) **2.** purchasing power **3.** optimum capacity **4.** assembly line (also called a *production line*) **5.** finished goods **6.** product recall **7.** offshore production **8.** planned obsolescence **9.** supply chain **10.** zero defects **11.** resource allocation **12.** raw materials **13.** manufacturing costs **14.** random sampling **15.** capacity planning

Exercise 2:
1. bar coding **2.** logistics **3.** preventive maintenance (also called *preventative* maintenance) **4.** intermediate goods **5.** stockout **6.** down time **7.** margin of error **8.** just in time (usually written *just-in-time*) **9.** made to order **10.** first in, first out (abbreviated to *FIFO*) **11.** supply and demand **12.** research and development (abbreviated to *R and D*) **13.** global pricing **14.** outsourcing **15.** continuous improvement **16.** spare parts

The phrase in the shaded vertical strip is **division of labour**.

Exercise 3:
There are a few combinations, but these are the best matches:
automatic assembly   batch production   buffer stock   buying manager   centralised purchasing   cluster sampling   contract manufacturing   forward scheduling   freight forwarder   list price   order book   paced line   quality control   shop floor (= factory floor, in a production / operations context)   surplus capacity

Recruitment 1: Job advertising (page 39)

1. leading **2.** vacancy **3.** post (we can also say *position* or *job*) **4.** commencing **5.** application (the verb is *to apply*) **6.** candidate (we can also say *applicant*) **7.** qualified **8.** experience **9.** team **10.** drive **11.** motivate (the noun is *motivation*, the adjective is *motivated*) **12.** colleagues (we sometimes use the informal word *workmates*) **13.** responsibilities (we can also say *duties*) **14.** rewards package (we can also say *benefits package*) **15.** basic salary (note that a *salary* is the money, or *pay*, you receive every month or year for doing your job; a *wage* is money you receive every <u>day</u> or <u>week</u> for doing a job: see the section on 'Rewards and benefits' elsewhere in this book for more information) **16.** commission **17.** incentive **18.** increment **19.** relocation allowance **20.** benefits (we can also say *rewards*) **21.** advance **22.** CV (= *curriculum vitae.* We can also say *resumé*. A CV lists your qualifications and experience in detail, and also provides important personal information - name, age, contact details, etc.) **23.** covering letter **24.** interview (A person <u>attending</u> an interview is called an *interviewee*; a person <u>conducting</u> an interview is called an *interviewer*)

Recruitment 2: The recruitment process (pages 40–41)

Part 1.
1. vacancy **2.** recruit **3.** staff **4.** internally (an *internal appointment*) **5.** externally **6.** appointments / situations vacant (informally called the *jobs pages* or *jobs section*) **7.** situations vacant / appointments **8.** journals **9.** recruitment agency **10.** institutional agency **11.** job centres **12.** private recruitment agency **13.** description **14.** applicants (from the verb *to apply*) **15.** qualifications **16.** experience **17.** personal qualities **18.** rewards (sometimes called *remuneration*) **19.** increments **20.** benefits **21.** leave (or *holiday*) **22.** discrimination **23.** equal opportunities **24.** affirmative recruitment **25.** disabilities

In Britain, the *Equal Opportunities Commission* (EOC) is the government body set up to make sure that no sex discrimination exists in employment. The *Commission for Racial Equality* (CRE) is the statutory body set up to *monitor* racial matters in companies, and to issue *guidelines* on best practice. Official *legislation* ensures that nobody is discriminated against (for example, the *Sex Discrimination Act* of 1975, the *Race Relations Act* of 1976, and the *Disability Discrimination Act* of 1995). Companies have a *vicarious liability* to ensure that discrimination is not a feature of the workplace.

Part 2.
1. CV (= *curriculum vitae*) **2.** covering **3.** introduction **4.** application **5.** pre-selection **6.** turn down **7.** short-list **8.** candidates **9.** one-to-one **10.** board **11.** psychometric **12.** aptitude (compare this with an *ability test*, which only tests the candidates current skills and knowledge) **13.** group situational **14.** in-basket **15.** medical (sometimes just called a *medical*) **16.** health screening

A test should have *face validity* - it should be relevant, useful and give accurate results that indicate how well the employee will perform.

Part 3.
1. seven-point plan   **2.** potential   **3.** appearance
4. intelligence   **5.** skills   **6.** interests   **7.** disposition
8. circumstances **9.** references **10.** offered   **11.** induction programme **12.** temporary **13.** probationary   **14.** open-ended / fixed-term   **15.** fixed-term / open-ended
16. follow-up

Recruitment 3: Contract of employment and job description (pages 42–43)

Exercise 1:
1. Term = Terms, conditionals = conditions   **2.** employ
= employer   **3.** employed = employee   **4.** titel = title
5. descriptive = description   **6.** locally = location   **7.** Celery
= Salary, anum = annum, rears = arrears   **8.** Started = Starting (or *Start*)   **9.** labour = work, until = to (*Monday through Friday* in American English)   **10.** Undertime = Overtime, rat = rate   **11.** enticement = entitlement, anum = annum   **12.** Absent = Absence (or *Absenteeism* ~~from work~~)   **13.** sceme = scheme (x2), employs = employees
14. Dissiplinary = Disciplinary, grieving = grievance, handybook = handbook, police = policies   **15.** Probbation
= Probation (x2), subjective = subject, employees
= employment, note = notice   **16.** Terminator
= Termination, probbation = probation (or probationary), note = notice   **17.** Referrals = References (x2) (a person who writes a reference is called a *referee*), apointments
= appointments   **18.** singed = signed

> Contracts of employment can be *temporary*, *permanent*, *short term*, *long term*, *fixed-term* or *open-ended*.
> Contracts contain *express terms* (those that both the employer and the employee agree on), and *implied terms* (these are *not* stated in the contract, but impose obligations on both the employer and the employee)
> Some contracts may contain a *restrictive covenant* (a clause which prevents an employee from doing something. For example, it may prevent the employee working for another similar company when s/he finishes work in his / her current company).
> *Contractual liability* is a legal responsibility for something as stated in a contract.

Exercise 2:
Here is the complete conversation:

James: Hi, Sarah. How's the new job going?
Sarah: Oh, not too bad. I'm still trying to find my feet, though.
James: Tell me a bit about it.
Sarah: Well, my official job **title** is Regional Production Manager, which means that my main **accountability** is to **supervise** the work of the production department.
James: Where are you **based**?
Sarah: Most of my work is done at the **head office** in central London, but I also have to spend time at our various **branches** and **departments** in the area. There are several of these in the South and South-East.
James: Who do you **report to**?
Sarah: The Central Production Manager. Tom Atkinson, his name is. I've only met him a couple of times, but he seems nice enough. We meet once a month to **consult** each other on major issues. We **evaluate** the current

state of production, and I **recommend** any changes that I think need to be made
James: And what about the **hours**?
Sarah: Pretty typical for this kind of job. I'm on a **full-time** contract, which means I work from Monday to Friday, **nine to five**. And occasionally I have to go in at the weekend, too. I get 21 days **leave** a year, plus bank holidays.
James: Not bad. And your **salary**? If you don't mind me asking?
Sarah: No, not at all. I get £35000 **per annum**, plus expenses, **commission** for reaching targets, overtime pay and so on.
James: That's pretty good for a job that just involves checking things are running smoothly.
Sarah: Well, there's more to my job than just that. I do have several other **key responsibilities**.
James: Such as?
Sarah: First of all I have to **agree** product specifications with sales departments and time schedules with the stock control department. Then I need to **ensure** that the product is manufactured according to agreed specifications, and I also have to **inspect** the quality of the finished product.
James: That's all?
Sarah: No. I also need to **negotiate** with our suppliers on prices for our base materials, **visit** those suppliers on a regular basis to check the quality of the base materials…
James: Do you have a car for that?
Sarah: Oh yes, the company provides me with one. I also have to **deal with** problems as they arise on a day-to-day basis, and **produce** regular sales reports for the Directors.
James: Anything else?
Sarah: Well, on top of everything else, I'm **responsible** for managing 10 machinists, 3 trainees, 2 cleaners and 2 security guards.
James: That sounds like a lot of work for one person. Can you **delegate** any of it?
Sarah: Unfortunately no. I have to do it all myself!

Sales and marketing 1 (pages 44–45)

1. cowded = crowded   **2.** nich = niche   **3.** uniqe
= unique   **4.** feachures = features   **5.** patient = patent
6. inovative = innovative   **7.** lunch = launch   **8.** brocure
= brochure   **9.** opmarket = upmarket   **10.** reserch
= research   **11.** advertiseing = advertising   **12.** campain
= campaign   **13.** premote = promote   **14.** comercials
= commercials   **15.** spouts = spots (an informal word)
16. advertisments = advertisements   **17.** pacement
= placement   **18.** billyboards = billboards (we can also say *hoardings*)   **19.** plop-ups = pop-ups   **20.** mailshoots
= mailshots   **21.** sponsership = sponsorship   **22.** endoarse
= endorse   **23.** opinon = opinion   **24.** pont = point
25. retale = retail   **26.** pich = pitch (an informal word)
27. miscounts = discounts   **28.** giveways = giveaways
29. dommestic = domestic   **30.** expot = export   **31.** raps
= reps (= short form of *representatives*)   **32.** franshise
= franchise   **33.** guarantea = guarantee   **34.** where
= wear (part of an expression: *wear and tear*)
35. merchantizing = merchandizing   **36.** brant = brand
37. loco = logo   **38.** pakaging = packaging   **39.** cattalog
= catalogue   **40.** hyp = hype   **41.** fat = fad
42. competiton = competition   **43.** tramp = trump (an informal word)   **44.** trucking = tracking   **45.** canvince
= convince

Answer key

Sales and marketing 2 (page 46)

1. obsolescence   **2.** Promotion (*promotion* is also the selling of a new product through the use of 'free gifts', by giving special discounts, etc)   **3.** Wholesale   **4.** benchmarking   **5.** Spam®   **6.** licensing   **7.** global   **8.** dealership   **9.** markdown   **10.** sampling   **11.** diversification   **12.** Telemarketing   **13.** distributor   **14.** freebie   **15.** airtime

The expression in the shaded vertical strip is **low-hanging fruit**.

Sales and marketing 3 (pages 47–48)

1. added value   **2.** trade fair   **3.** brand loyalty   **4.** focus group   **5.** break even   **6.** reward scheme   **7.** price war (also called a *price-cutting war*)   **8.** white goods   **9.** mailing house   **10.** product differentiation   **11.** customer care   **12.** cold call   **13.** crisis management   **14.** client base (also called a *client list*)   **15.** network marketing   **16.** loss leader   **17.** sales forecast   **18.** high pressure   **19.** brand awareness   **20.** public relations   **21.** market leader   **22.** press release   **23.** price insensitive   **24.** product abandonment   **25.** consumer protection   **26.** trade delegation   **27.** corporate image   **28.** price leadership   **29.** target market   **30.** premium offer   **31.** own brand   **32.** market driven

Note that, as with other exercises in this book, these words are not always exclusive to the area of sales and marketing, and may be relevant to other business areas.

Similar meanings 1: Nouns (pages 49–50)

Exercise 1:
1. agenda / schedule   **2.** administration / receivership   **3.** discipline / order   **4.** takeover / acquisition   **5.** drop / decline   **6.** faults / defects   **7.** opposition / resistance   **8.** proof / evidence   **9.** discount / reduction   **10.** proximity / closeness   **11.** appointment / meeting   **12.** customers / clients   **13.** work / employment   **14.** benefits / advantages   **15.** requirements / prerequisites   **16.** acclaim / praise   **17.** code / rules   **18.** liability / responsibility   **19.** choices / options   **20.** staff / personnel   **21.** cooperation / collaboration   **22.** charisma / (personal) appeal

Exercise 2:
1. reviews / write-ups   **2.** advertising / publicity   **3.** customers / patrons   **4.** categories / classifications (we could also use *plans* here)   **5.** ending / termination   **6.** entitlement / rights   **7.** calibre / intellect and ability   **8.** specialist / expert   **9.** assignment / job   **10.** notion / idea   **11.** proficiency / skill   **12.** achievement / accomplishment   **13.** ultimatum / final demand   **14.** disparity / difference   **15.** proceeds / earnings   **16.** terms / conditions   **17.** questions / queries   **18.** outlets / shops   **19.** problems / complications   **20.** strategy / plan   **21.** priority / precedence   **22.** revisions / changes

Similar meanings 2: Verbs (pages 51–52)

Across: **4.** assist   **9.** consent   **11.** clarify   **12.** reserve   **13.** regulate   **14.** analyse   **16.** gather   **17.** address   **24.** select   **26.** generate   **28.** administer   **30.** confirm   **33.** audit   **34.** brief   **35.** relate   **37.** quantify   **39.** deduct   **41.** oblige   **42.** widen   **43.** employ

Down: **1.** finalise   **2.** imply   **3.** consult   **4.** accelerate   **5.** handle   **6.** retain   **7.** attend   **8.** convey   **9.** compensate   **10.** disclose   **12.** resolve   **15.** substitute   **18.** dictate   **19.** assert   **20.** advertise   **21.** avert   **22.** deplete   **23.** reclaim   **25.** endorse   **27.** prohibit   **29.** influence   **31.** award   **32.** attempt   **36.** ascertain   **38.** acquire   **40.** explain

Similar meanings 3: Adjectives (pages 53-54)

Exercise 1:
1. extensive   **2.** mandatory   **3.** resolute   **4.** adequate   **5.** inconsistent   **6.** thorough   **7.** overall   **8.** scrupulous   **9.** discourteous   **10.** restricted   **11.** vibrant   **12.** outdated   **13.** abundant   **14.** pertinent   **15.** inflexible   **16.** risky   **17.** basic   **18.** narrow   **19.** abrupt   **20.** crucial

Exercise 2:
1. prospective   **2.** enduring   **3.** rudimentary   **4.** thriving   **5.** voluntary   **6.** tedious   **7.** steady   **8.** disparate   **9.** profitable   **10.** lengthy   **11.** nominal   **12.** integral   **13.** exceptional   **14.** compatible   **15.** perceptive   **16.** punctual   **17.** legitimate   **18.** industrious   **19.** disciplinary   **20.** inventive   **21.** important   **22.** modern   **23.** diverse   **24.** efficient   **25.** flexible   **26.** bankrupt

On the telephone (pages 55–56)

Exercise 1:
1. engaged / call...back   **2.** put...through / Hold the line   **3.** connect / message / voicemail / convenient   **4.** automated services / zeroing out (= pressing the zero key in the hope that you will speak to someone) / dead / cut off   **5.** tone / get...back   **6.** on hold / camping on the line (= waiting on hold or a long time)   **7.** junk calls (= *unsolicited cold calls* from companies trying to sell you something)   **8.** Speaking (= *I am the person you want to speak to*) / on behalf of / hung up   **9.** extension / direct line / switchboard / hang on   **10.** star (= *) / hash (= #)

Exercise 2:
1. as a matter of fact   **2.** as soon as possible   **3.** be right back   **4.** by the way   **5.** for crying out loud (= an exclamation of frustration and anger)   **6.** for what it's worth (= an expression used when giving your opinion about something, usually to someone who has received some bad news and you are trying to make them feel a bit better)   **7.** ha ha only kidding (humorous. *Kidding = joking*)   **8.** hope this helps   **9.** I am not a lawyer (used humorously when someone asks you a complicated question, especially about legal matters)   **10.** in my opinion   **11.** in other words   **12.** keep it simple, stupid (humorous. It can also mean *keep it short and simple*)   **13.** my eyes glaze over (humorous, used for saying that something is extremely boring)   **14.** mind your own business (usually humorous)   **15.** on the other hand   **16.** with respect to

Note that, sometimes, abbreviations use letters that are not used at the beginning of the word, but are instead pronounced like the word itself. For example, 'CUL' means '*See you later*'. Numbers are also used to represent words or parts of words. For example, 'UR2L8' means '*You are too late*'.

• When we <u>say</u> telephone numbers, we usually speak each number individually. For example: *020 7837 7324* is usually spoken as '*Oh two oh / seven eight three seven / seven three two four*'.
• If a number is doubled, we normally say '*double*' before it. For example: *0845 601 5884* is usually spoken as '*Oh eight four five / six oh one / five <u>double</u> eight four*'
• If a telephone number has one or more zeros after a number, and no numbers after it, we often say it as one number. For example: *0800 <u>800</u> 151* is often spoken as '*Oh <u>eight hundred</u> / <u>eight hundred</u> / one five one*'.
• Six-figure numbers are becoming increasingly spoken as three separate numbers. For example: *0800 <u>201215</u>* is spoken '*Oh eight hundred / <u>twenty</u> / <u>twelve</u> / <u>fifteen</u>*'.

Trade (pages 57–58)

Here are the complete sentences, with the answers in **bold**.

• When you bring goods into a country you **import** them. When you send them out of a country you **export** them.
• A group of manufacturers or suppliers who visit another country to increase their sales there is known as a trade **delegation**.
• **Cargo** - also called **freight** - is a general word for goods which are transported in a ship, plane etc. It is usually carried in a **container** (= a very large metal case of a standard size).
• A bill of **lading** is a list of goods being transported, which the transporter gives to the person sending the goods, to show them that the goods have been loaded. The person receiving the goods should receive a **packing** list, showing them the goods that they should be receiving.
• A letter of **credit** - often abbreviated to *L/C* - is a document issued by a bank on behalf of a customer authorising payment to a supplier when conditions specified in the document are met.
• A **pro-forma** invoice is an invoice sent to a buyer before the goods are sent, so that payment can be made (or so that goods can be sent to a consignee who is not the buyer).
• *COD* is a payment which is made for goods when they arrive. *COD* stands for *cash on **delivery***.
• A group of goods sent for sale by road, sea or air is called a **consignment**.
• *CIF* refers to the price a buyer has to pay for goods which have to be transported. It stands for ***cost**, **insurance** and freight*.
• Goods sent by air are called **airfreight**. Goods sent by sea are called **seafreight**.
• FOB stand for *free on **board***. It refers to the price a buyer pays a seller for goods. The price includes all the seller's costs until the goods are on the ship, plane, etc, for transportation.
• Import **duty** - also sometimes called an import **levy** - is a tax which has to be paid on goods coming into a country. A customs **tariff** is a list of those taxes that must be paid.
• A person or company which arranges shipping and **customs** documents is called a **forwarding** agent.
• If tax on imported goods is not paid, those goods may be **impounded** (in other words, they are kept in a secure **warehouse** at or near the **port** of entry until that tax is paid).
• A **clearing** agent arranges the import and delivery of goods at their port of **destination**.

• As soon as goods are allowed into a country by the customs officer, we can say that they have been **cleared**.
• A record of the international trading position of a country in **merchandise** (= goods), excluding invisible trade, is called the ***balance** of trade*.
• A **wholesale** price is a price paid by customers (for example, shops) who buy goods in large quantities. They sell these goods to individual customers (for example, shoppers) at a higher price which is called the **retail** price. Some offer **discounts** to their customers, which means they pay a little less
• A **licensing** agreement allows a company to market or produce goods or services owned by another company, and is a popular means for a company to penetrate the overseas market.
• A **quota** is a limited amount of a good that can be brought into a country (usually as an incentive for people to buy home-produced versions of that good). This is an example of a trade **barrier**.
• When goods are sold within one country, they are transported to their place of sale by a **distributor**.

Business travel (pages 59–60)

Exercise 1:
1. delayed   **2.** overbooked   **3.** tourist *or* coach *or* economy   **4.** embarkation *or* boarding   **5.** transit   **6.** gate   **7.** non-stop (a *direct flight* may land somewhere between its departure point and its destination, although the passengers do not need to change planes, and may not even need to leave the plane they are on. For example, a direct flight from London to Singapore may land, or *stop over*, in Dubai for a couple of hours)   **8.** domestic   **9.** single *or* one-way / return trip *or* round-trip   **10.** credit limit   **11.** crew   **12.** commuters   **13.** carrier *or* airline   **14.** comprehensive   **15.** 4x4 (pronounced *four by four*, also called an *SUV*)

Exercise 2:
1. schedule *or* itinerary   **2.** trip (*voyage* does not really work here, as this word usually refers to a long journey by land or sea)   **3.** valid (*validate* is a verb)   **4.** runs out *or* expires (although *expires* is a better word)   **5.** visa   **6.** embassy   **7.** traveller's cheques   **8.** currency   **9.** exchange   **10.** deal   **11.** commission   **12.** insurance   **13.** vaccinations   **14.** provider   **15.** network

Exercise 3:
1. At the airport (at the *check-in desk*) or at a hotel (when you *check into* your room)   **2.** Your baggage weighs more than the allowed amount, and so you have to pay extra money for the airline to carry it   **3.** Your flight has been overbooked (see number 2 in Exercise 1) and your seat has been given to someone else   **4.** You want to move to a higher class of travel (for example, from economy class to business class)   **5.** Transport from the airport to your hotel or another place at your destination   **6.** No. Passengers flying between countries in the EU (the *European Union*) are not allowed a duty free allowance (ie, alcohol, cigarettes, perfume, etc, on which a special tax has to be paid)   **7.** fare   **8.** A ticket for a journey (especially one by aircraft) which is stored in a computer and is not given to the passenger (who usually has a receipt for the ticket instead)   **9.** No. Jet lag is usually experienced by people flying from west to east, and vice versa. Cape Town is in the same time zone as London, so passengers should not be affected by time changes   **10.** *Full board* accommodation means that the price of

Answer key

your room includes all meals; *half board* includes room, breakfast and your evening meal; *bed and breakfast* (*B and B*) includes your room and breakfast only.   **11.** A *single room* has one small bed, a *twin room* has two small beds, a *double room* has one large bed, a *suite* has one large bed and will also have a separate area with a sofa, armchair, etc, for relaxing   **12.** The full price for staying in a room, with no discount   **13.** (a) housekeeping, (b) reception, (c) maintenance, (d) switchboard, (e) room service, (f) concierge   **14.** wardrobe, safe, mini bar, balcony, air conditioning, tea and coffee facilities, Internet access, iron, television, remote control (for the television and / or air conditioning)   **15.** Probably not: the adjectives in italics are negative   **16.** In many situations where a service is provided, such as in a taxi, in a restaurant, at a hairdresser, at a hotel when the porter carries your bags to your room, etc.

Word association (page 61)

1. pension   **2.** business   **3.** job   **4.** price   **5.** corporate   **6.** cost   **7.** tax   **8.** industrial   **9.** minimum   **10.** salary   **11.** strike   **12.** shift   **13.** management   **14.** health   **15.** labour   **16.** employment   **17.** insurance   **18.** career   **19.** market   **20.** income   **21.** customer   **22.** private   **23.** staff   **24.** group   **25.** contract   **26.** sales   **27.** personal   **28.** brand

Working hours and time off work (pages 62–64)

Exercise 1:
1. time-keeping   **2.** allowed time   **3.** job-share   **4.** flexitime   **5.** flexileader   **6.** flexilagger   **7.** unsocial hours   **8.** full-time   **9.** part-time   **10.** double time   **11.** time and a half   **12.** overtime   **13.** core time   **14.** shift transfer   **15.** fixed hours   **16.** rotating shifts   **17.** graveyard shift   **18.** homeworking (people who do this are sometimes referred to as *open-collar workers*)   **19.** roster   **20.** clock off (used informally even if you do not use a card and machine: "*Right, that's it. I'm clocking off for the day*". We can also say *clock out*. When we arrive for work we *clock on* or *clock in*)   **21.** time sheet   **22.** Flexible Work Regulations (see note *1 below)   **23.** work-life balance (see note *2 below)   **24.** shift differentials   **25.** twilight shift   **26.** job rotation

*1: In Britain, the *Working Time Directive* of 1998 (based on guidelines set by the European Union) sets out the following regulations: Employees should work no more than 48 hours a week, and should receive a minimum of 4 weeks' paid leave a year. They should have a weekly rest period of at least 24 consecutive hours, a daily break of at least 20 minutes for every six hours worked, and a daily rest period of 11 consecutive hours. There are different directives for some groups (e.g., pilots, bus drivers, doctors, etc) whose jobs are more stressful, demand greater concentration, or whose performance might affect other people.

*2: *Work-life balance* is the subject of widespread debate on how to allow employees more control over their working arrangements so that they have more time for their outside activities and responsibilities, but in a way that will still benefit the organisations they work for. Flexible working practices and family-friendly policies are two areas of work-life balance that are frequently the focus of debate.

Exercise 2:
1. medical (also called a *doctor's certificate*)   **2.** statutory (SSP = *statutory sick pay*)   **3.** maternity   **4.** unpaid   **5.** gardening   **6.** sabbatical (this word is especially used for teachers, university professors, etc, who take time away from their school or college)   **7.** absenteeism   **8.** public holiday (called a *bank holiday* in the UK, and a *legal holiday* in the USA)   **9.** long-service   **10.** entitlement   **11.** unauthorised (also spelt *unauthorized*. An employee who takes unauthorised leave *is* or *goes AWOL*: *absent without leave*)   **12.** waiting   **13.** absence   **14.** in lieu (usually abbreviated to *TOIL*)   **15.** paternity   **16.** casual   **17.** vacation   **18.** benefit

The expression in the shaded vertical strip is **compassionate leave**.

Workplace problems (pages 65–66)

Exercise 1:
Paragraph (A) **1.** dispute   **2.** resolved   **3.** strike   **4.** arbitrate
Paragraph (B) **1.** fraud   **2.** discrimination   **3.** bullying   **4.** racial   **5.** abuse   **6.** sexual   **7.** harassment   **8.** fired   **9.** suspended   **10.** unfair   **11.** dismissal (we can also say *wrongful dismissal*)   **12.** appeal
Paragraph (C) **1.** breaches   **2.** neglecting (this can also be a noun: *neglect* of duties)   **3.** insubordination   **4.** damage   **5.** disciplinary   **6.** board   **7.** instant   **8.** dismissal   **9.** zero tolerance
Paragraph (D) **1.** shortages   **2.** overstretched   **3.** grievance   **4.** walkout   **5.** verbal   **6.** warning (after a *verbal warning*, an employee might receive a *written warning*)   **7.** notice (when a company *asks you for your notice*, they are politely telling you that they are going to force you to resign)
Paragraph (E) **1.** dropped   **2.** redundant   **3.** resigned   **4.** bankrupt   **5.** hacked   **6.** virus   **7.** crashed   **8.** order (*out of order* = broken / not working)
Paragraph (F) **1.** plateauing   **2.** stimulation   **3.** motivation   **4.** initiative   **5.** productivity   **6.** implement
Paragraph (G) **1.** turnover   **2.** retention   **3.** conflict   **4.** absenteeism   **5.** timekeeping   **6.** misconduct   **7.** morale   **8.** industrial   **9.** counsel   **10.** grievances

Exercise 2:
1. absenteeism   **2.** plateauing   **3.** counsel   **4.** turnover   **5.** redundant   **6.** dispute   **7.** overstretched   **8.** arbitrate   **9.** discrimination   **10.** harassment   **11.** grievance   **12.** motivation   **13.** misconduct   **14.** breach   **15.** walkout   **16.** initiative   **17.** insubordination (usually used in a work environment where there are strict rules and a strict hierarchy)   **18.** appeal   **19.** verbal   **20.** implement   **21.** notice   **22.** morale

207380